Tales from Jackpine Bob

Tales from Jackpine Bob

Written and Illustrated by Bob Cary

University of Minnesota Press
Minneapolis / London

Published by the University of Minnesota Press
111 Third Avenue South, Suite 290
Minneapolis, MN 55401-2520
http://www.upress.umn.edu

ISBN 0-8166-4394-6 (PB)

A Cataloging-in-Publication record for this book is available
from the Library of Congress.

Printed in the United States of America on acid-free paper

The University of Minnesota is an equal-opportunity educator
and employer.

11 10 09 08 07 06 05 04 03   10 9 8 7 6 5 4 3 2 1

Dedication

It is, they say in literary circles, proper to dedicate a book to someone who has had a profound influence on the author's work or life. In this respect, no one has had a more profound influence on my life and work than my mother, Cornelia Cary, who is preparing to celebrate her 101st birthday at the time of this writing. Her good humor, courage, kindness, dedication to honesty, and perseverance have been an inspiration to her family and to all who know her. As a gentle critic and unabashed supporter of my writing, she had much to do in shaping my career. It is to my mother I dedicate this book.

Contents

Acknowledgment

During the preparation of this book, much of the computer work, printouts, and original copy reading were done by my friend Ann Wognum, publisher of the *Ely Echo* newspaper. To her I owe a debt of gratitude.

Foreword

Among the people of the Ojibwa First Nation, there is a belief that the northern forest is inhabited by invisible, irascible little folk called Memegawish, who take delight in hiding knives, canoe paddles, teapots, and other possessions of unwary human visitors to the wilderness. The Ojibwa say: "You cannot see the little folk, but if you are sitting by the fire at night and you listen very closely, you can hear them in the treetops laughing at the tricks they played on you." Over many years on many forest trails, my wife—a quarter Indian—and I have heard the laughter and joined in with it. I hope that you may listen by your fire, and laugh with them too.

Bob Cary
1995

A Touch of Class

Over forty-six years of marriage, Lil and I never really fought about anything. Sure, we had some arguments, but no real fights. Except once over deer hunting. It had to do with deer scent, the smelly stuff you put on either to mask the human odor that spooks deer or to attract deer to your stand. Only my wife refused to wear deer scent.

Things came to a head in the 1987 season. I arrived home one evening before the season and handed her two small plastic bottles.

"What's this?" she asked, suspiciously.

"Deer scent. Two kinds. One is Buck Scent and the other is Doe in Heat."

She quickly handed the two bottles back.

"Listen," I said. "Those bucks have great olfactory senses. They can smell you a quarter mile away."

"I don't care. I'm not dabbing that junk on my hunting clothes."

I found from long experience that when my wife did not want to do something, she likely wouldn't do it. I put the bottles on the fireplace mantel with our rifle clips and thought she might have a change of heart on opening day.

It didn't happen. Opening morning I was off and gone as she was pouring her first cup of coffee. "Hey . . . I'll be mooching around

1

the woods until afternoon," I said. "Then I'll work my way over to your stand . . . so keep awake."

"I'm always awake," she responded, tartly.

"And take some of that scent along. You've gotta have scent to get a big buck."

"Baloney."

I headed for the woods, wondering why the Lord created women so contrary. But it was a nice day. Four inches of fresh tracking snow covered the ground, creating perfect conditions. Several times I kicked deer out of the thickets, but none wearing antlers. In the late afternoon, I came on a huge scrape and a set of pony-sized tracks. "Whooee," I thought. "Here's a trophy!" Carefully I began to stalk the big boy, easing along silently, stopping to watch ahead and to each side. The tracks led directly down a trail winding toward Lil's deer stand located on a little ridge overlooking a brushy ravine. Something told me I should be hearing a rifle shot any time, but as I came over the last rise before the ravine, I saw where the big buck had slammed on the brakes, paused for a moment, then moved off laterally 90 degrees from the trail. Somewhat disgusted, I strode on up to Lil's deer stand. She poked her orange cap up from the balsam cover.

"Hi." She grinned.

"Hi yourself. I had one coming your way, but it spooked," I growled. "Did you have any of that deer scent on?"

"No. You know I'm not going to wear that stuff."

"Listen. This was a big buck. A real big one. He would've come in, I'm sure, but he winded you and veered off. You've gotta wear scent to get a big buck."

"Stop bugging me."

That night in the cabin, I started to take up the argument again. "Listen!" Lil snarled at me. "I read the labels on those bottles. They've got deer pee and Lord knows what else in there. You don't think I am going to dab myself with deer pee, do you?"

I was getting a little red around the neck. "Well, I'm getting doggone tired of chasing deer around the woods," I said hotly, "just to have them spook out every time they get near your deer stand."

"Nuts."

We went to bed early without saying much to each other. Got up in the dark in about the same mood. I shoved down some bacon and eggs, checked my watch, and picked the .30-06 off the rack.

"Wear some scent today, for cripes sake," I said with finality. "You can't get a big buck without scent."

Lil gave me a dirty look as I went out the door. It was maddening. If there was ever a case for justifiable homicide, this was it. The day didn't amount to much, either. Up hill, down dale. Mile on mile. Heard a few deer running, but saw nothing, not even a doe. Very late in the afternoon, as the sun was skidding into the spruce and balsam, I circled back down the old trail and picked up another big track. Looked like the same old buck. Heading down the same way. Right over the tracks from the day before. I was hurrying along before it got too dark, when the boom of Lil's rifle shattered the silence like a cannon going off. I started to jog ahead, coming out within sight of the deer stand. Lil was part way down toward the ravine. She waved her rifle and with the other hand signaled "thumbs up." Lying in the snow at her feet was a dandy buck, a massive stag with ten polished points on his rack.

"Nice shot," I said, noting the single hole behind the right shoulder.

"Thanks. He came right in."

I quickly dressed out the animal, finishing in the glare of Lil's flashlight. With his front feet lashed to the antlers, we skidded him to the road with the drag rope, then hiked to the cabin, got in the van, and drove back. With the buck loaded up, we headed for town and the official state big game registration station. It weighed 210 pounds, even. Pretty hefty trophy.

From there we drove over to Vertin's Cafe, ordered burgers and coffee. "Pretty darn nice buck," I reiterated. Success had thoroughly dispelled the anger of the morning.

"Yeah. Thanks for driving him into me." Lil reached over and patted my arm.

I thought for a moment, then decided to put the question. "Did you have the scent on?"

"You bet," she said with enthusiasm.

I was somewhat startled, but asserted my righteousness. "See . . . what'd I tell you. Gotta have scent to get a big buck."

"Right!" Lil agreed.

When we got home, I hung the deer in the woodshed, came in, and washed my hands. "See what I told you," I continued. "You got to wear scent to get a big buck."

"You bet," she said with a big smile.

Next morning, I was getting dressed by lamplight. Lil watched from the bed." You going out?" I asked.

"No. I got mine. You go get your own. And don't forget the scent."

She pulled the covers up and went back to sleep.

All day I hiked up and down the ridges but saw only a couple of small does. About two in the afternoon, heading toward the road, I picked up three tracks, one of which looked like it might be a buck, angling toward Lil's deer stand. I hoped she had a change of heart and was back in there, but no such luck. The tracks went up the trail, but instead of going past the stand, went right up to the old balsam-covered wood frame. The three animals had circled the deer stand, and the biggest track indicated that the deer had leaned over for a look inside. Incredible. I had never seen anything like that!

I legged it home, somewhat mystified, and told Lil about the deer. "Did you sprinkle some scent inside the stand?" I asked.

"Yeah . . . what I didn't put on my cap and jacket."

"Which kind did you use?"

"Whatta you mean?"

"Which scent? The Doe in Heat or the Buck Scent?"

"Neither one."

"Neither?"

"No, I told you I wasn't going to put any deer pee on my clothes."

"You said you used scent."

"I did." Lil went into the bedroom, rummaged for a moment, and came back out with a small glass bottle she handed to me. I looked at the label. It read: "Faberge." And below that: "A Touch of Class."

"Perfume?"

"You didn't expect me to wear deer pee, did you?"

For a moment I was stunned. Then I said: "You used perfume to bring that buck in? And that's what those other deer were attracted to?"

"Sure, why don't you try some?"

"I can't."

"Why not?"

"What if I run into another hunter? What's he going to think if I smell like women's perfume?"

"Well, that's your problem, but I'll tell you one thing."

"What's that?"

"You've gotta wear scent if you want to get a big buck," she giggled.

The Fifteen-Horse Motor

It was the summer of 1933, the summer my father and Spang's father took us fishing at Red Cedar Lake. The expedition had been in the planning stage since before school let out at Farragut Junior High, a great stone edifice where Spang and I were incarcerated in the seventh grade.

"Take about a whole day to drive there, Paul," Pop said, "barring flats and engine trouble on the Model A."

"We could make it faster with my new Oakland," Spang's pop said. "Besides, Rex, we'd have more room in my sedan for the kids and the suitcases."

The fact that we were being considered as fellow participants in this search for the angling Holy Grail had Spang and me in a state of nervous expectation. Back nearly as long as we could remember, we had heard stories of Red Cedar Lake, stories our fathers had spun over cold glasses of contraband on late summer nights (Prohibition was still in force). Wide-eyed, we absorbed tales of huge bass that lay in shadowy ambush beneath the green lily-pad cover, of saw-toothed pike that shredded fish lines and broke rods at the handle.

And then there were the photos, snapshots of our fathers in knickers and straw hats, posing with cigarettes dangling carelessly from the corners of their mouths, holding up vast stringers of gleaming fish. Real man stuff. Now, finally, at age twelve, we were scheduled to go with them.

As the date of our departure drew near, preparations became intense. Every item of tackle had to be gone over again and again. Extra clothes were packed and repacked. With flashlights, Spang and I spent several nights on neighborhood lawns capturing nightcrawlers—long, slippery members of the genus *Lumbricus*, also known as "dew worms." In Spang's basement we had a wooden crate filled with damp moss, a box with escape-proof sides and top, where more than two hundred worms were kept.

The night before we left, our mothers went over our suitcases to see that everything necessary, like toothbrushes and handkerchiefs, was included. As a final gesture, Spang's pop and mine presented us each with new, black, tubular steel rods with glass eyes, and well-used but still serviceable hand-me-down, chrome-plated reels that spun with a flick of a finger.

Sleep that night was impossible. Indeed, I kept slipping out of bed to look at the living room clock, amazed that it seemed to barely edge its way toward the magic hour of 5 A.M., when we would be up for breakfast and on our way. Ten minutes before the alarm went off, I was turning on the kitchen lights. Mom came out looking sleepy, but got busy frying eggs while Pop and I hauled our suitcases and tackle over to the four-door Oakland parked by Spang's house. Light was barely breaking in the east when we said good-bye, our dads wasting precious time kissing their wives. Finally we got on the ribbon of highway heading north.

In a roadside diner at noon, our dads went over the highway map, slapping each other on the back. "We're makin' darn good time, Paul," Pop said.

"Yeah, we're more'n halfway, Rex," Spang's dad acknowledged.

Half awake, Spang and I munched down our barbecues and

slurped our root beer. Our exuberance had been significantly eroded by lack of sleep the night before plus a July temperature soaring into the nineties. We dozed fitfully in the back seat most of the afternoon as the car swerved and bumped along, slowing down for speed limit signs at every little town and village. At 5 P.M., after twelve hours on the road, we were jolted awake as the car careened into a dusty lane and past a weathered wooden sign reading "Smith's Resort."

We were there!

Fatigue vanished like magic. Spang and I ran to the lakeshore, took in the sparkling blue expanse rimmed by pine and birch, the worn wooden dock and boathouse. Our host, George Smith, and his wife, Angie, helped us to our quarters, a cabin made of cedar logs, with two small bedrooms, a living room with one table and three scarred chairs, and a screened porch. An enameled basin and water pitcher on a stand composed the vanity ensemble, and a path in back led to our toilet, a wooden privy with a half-moon design sawed in the door. To Spang and me it was a Waldorf in the pines.

Meals, we were told, were served at seven, noon, and six in the lodge dining hall, a spacious log edifice that had originally housed an army of hungry lumberjacks during white-pine logging operations some four decades earlier. The interior was simple but clean, the rough wooden tables sheathed in well-laundered red-and-white covers.

The last items to check out were at the dock. Alongside a dozen smaller fishing craft was a sleek sixteen-foot cedar-strip boat and fifteen-horsepower outboard, both of which belonged to my great-uncle Albert. A rather successful newspaper publisher, he kept his craft stowed at this resort, a hideaway where he could occasionally escape from the hectic world of headlines and finance. The outboard motor, Pop allowed, was the biggest in current production, a gleaming chrome-and-enamel marvel of engineering with a seahorse painted on the gas tank. And Uncle Albert had given Pop express permission for us to use his boat.

Tired as we were, Spang and I slept only fitfully that night, geared up to the morrow's adventure. Our fathers had gone over a detailed lake map carefully with the lodge owner, marking in some of the bays, rocky points, and weedbeds that had been most productive of late. Our four rods leaned against the porch screen, strung up with leaders, hooks, and sinkers. Ready to go.

At the clang of the breakfast bell, we bolted for the dining room, where we loaded up on pancakes, syrup, and sausage, coffee for the men, brimming glasses of cold milk for Spang and me. And then down to the dock in feverish anticipation.

It was quickly and satisfactorily apparent that we had the hottest boat-and-motor combination on the lake. A half dozen other craft left the dock when we did, most of them powered with three-horse or five-horse "kickers" that we left bobbing in our wake. We were five miles away in the choice fishing spots with our lines in the water before any of the other boats came in sight.

Whoever the gods of fishing may be, they often smile on small boys, and sometimes on accompanying fathers. They smiled that day, multiplying our good fortune so that we came in for lunch with an impressive catch, one we held up while our host snapped several pictures with Pop's Kodak. The afternoon was a similar success, but after I hooked and landed more and bigger fish than I had ever seen before, my interest slowly switched over to that magnificent outboard motor.

"Lemme run the motor back to the resort, Pop?" I inquired at length.

"What?" Pop grabbed a fresh nightcrawler out of the container and carefully impaled it on his hook.

"Kin I run the motor back to the dock?"

"No. Now mind your fishin'."

"Well, just leave me run it a little way . . . "

"No! For cripes sake, you don't need to run the motor. Anyway, you're too young."

The next day, I started out a little earlier, pleading in my most plaintive manner to at least drive it a few miles up the lake. Pop was getting visibly red under the collar. "Listen. You button up on that motor stuff, you hear? Any more and you can stay in the cabin."

I knew from experience he wasn't kidding; but I also knew from experience that sometimes "no" meant "maybe."

After supper Spang whispered to me: "Do you think he'll let you run the motor?"

"I dunno," I whispered back, "but I'd give a million bucks to drive it down the lake just one time."

"Me, too," Spang muttered, aware that his chances were far slimmer than mine.

I let the subject cool the third day, but on the fourth day, I started it up again in the late afternoon, following one more successful foray into the realm of bass and walleyes. I sensed it was a good time because Pop had just boated a bass he bet would "go over six pounds," a real whopper with red eyes, dark brown back, jut underjaw, and flaring red gills. Pop held his trophy aloft while he quoted at length from the eminent bass authority of that day, Dr. James Henshall: "Inch-for-inch and pound-for-pound, the gamest fish that swims," Pop said. Paul nodded in solemn agreement.

In his moment of triumph, I again entreated: "Kin I run the motor back?"

Pop stopped his oration and glared at me. "Geez, if you aren't a beaut!" But as he slipped the big bass onto the stringer, he softened up a little. "Well . . . O.K. I'll start it, and you can steer it . . . but just back to the dock."

Spang turned frog green with envy as I slipped onto the broad stern seat. Pop wrapped the starter rope around the flywheel, opened the gas valve, set the throttle at "start" and gave it a little choke. On the second pull it sputtered and roared into motion. There were no such things as gear shifts on those early motors. When one started, it was in gear, so care was taken not to get the throttle very far open or the operator might take a high dive over the transom.

Pop shoved the choke shut as the motor warmed up, and I took over, holding the steering arm with my left hand and edging the throttle forward a little at a time with my right. A slight chop on the lake caused foam to curl away from the bow in two glorious cascades. In short order, I passed three other boats, my lip curling with disdain at their feeble attempts to match our speed. Reasonably sure things were under control, Pop swung around, shifting to the center seat and lifting the stringer so he could admire his bass at length. Spang sat alongside him, looking resolutely ahead as though he didn't give a hoot about me driving the boat, but I knew he was eating his heart out. Spang's old man sat on the front seat, back to the wind, facing toward me. He wore a somewhat worried look, occasionally swiveling around to peer at other boats ahead, then quickly glancing back to see if I was paying attention. I certainly was.

All too soon we were approaching the resort dock, and my euphoria began to dissipate. "Throttle down," Pop ordered, and I cut back on our speed.

It was at this point that things began to unravel. Smith's Resort, like many of that era, did not have small, individual docks where boats were tied up for loading and unloading. Smith's dock was a large, floating platform of logs and planks upon which the boats were pulled. When all the boats were on the dock, the lake end was partially submerged. And when a boat was needed for use, it was simply skidded off into the water.

One thing I had particularly noticed the first three days at the resort: when the professional guides brought their boats in, they didn't unload their guests and then pull their boats up on the planks;

instead, they aimed the bow at the dock, gunned the motor, and deftly drove the boat up on the planks.

In a burst of overconfidence, I determined to do the same, but I failed to indicate this to anyone else in our boat. Thus, as I approached the floating platform and lined up with it, the rest of my crew was making ready to step out. Spang's old man, who was rather portly to begin with, struggled to his feet, back to the dock, and reached down for his fishing rod. Timing our approach, I gave the throttle a twist, sharply accelerating the boat. Pop and Spang teetered backward on their seats, and Spang's old man almost fell on his face. We hit the floating dock full force, the boat leaping up on the planks exactly as I had seen the guide's boats do. At that point our forward progress came to an abrupt halt. Spang's old man now reversed direction and went flying over the seat backward.

Unfortunately, while we were fishing, he had his tackle box wide open, one of those huge metal affairs with multiple trays, profusely inhabited with various multihooked lures. With a roar of pain, he landed tail-end-first on the tackle box, legs flailing in the air. My father swiveled around, seething, a veritable tornado of anger. With my own death appearing imminent, I did the only sensible thing: I jumped over the side of the boat, hit the dock running, dashed up the stairway, past the cabins, and fled into the sanctuary of the nearby forest.

Once sufficiently back in the woods where pursuit was improbable, I sat down on a log, panting. My hands shook as I wiped sweat from my face and attempted to take stock. Obviously, there was no point in returning. My fate was sealed. What had been my greatest triumph had somehow disintegrated into ignominious disaster. I was certain my father would kill me the minute he got his hands on me.

I don't know exactly how long I sat on the log. The sun began descending in the west, and the shadows lengthened in the forest. Squadrons of insects began roaring up from the understory, intent on impaling every square inch of exposed flesh. In my somewhat disoriented condition, I was dimly aware that there were probably only two avenues to follow: I could run away and join the circus, or I could join the French Foreign Legion—either agency reportedly took volunteers from anywhere, no questions asked. However, in addition to the insect torment, my stomach was now complaining loudly that suppertime had long come and gone. Hunger and thirst were acute.

Perhaps, I reasoned, if I sneaked in the back door of the lodge kitchen, I might find some leftover tidbits from supper lying about, something to tide me over until I could make more substantial plans for the circus or the Legion. With that in mind, I fled the mosquito-infested woods and tiptoed silently up to the screened door of the lodge kitchen. As I prepared to slip through the door, I heard voices inside and considerable laughter. Pressing my ear to the screen, I clearly recognized my father's voice.

"Lord, you should have seen it, girls!" he roared. "The kid brought that boat up to the dock, and Paul stood up, expecting to step out . . . " Pop went off into a spasm of laughter. I opened the door a crack and saw he was talking to the cook and the waitresses.

"Well," he continued, "the darn kid opened the throttle, the boat shot forward, slammed the boards and stopped. Paul went tail over teakettle across the boat seat and landed smack in the middle of his open tackle box!" Pop slapped his legs, gasping. "Omigod! He came up outta there with all those lures decorating his rear end like a Christmas tree!" Pop, the cook, and the waitresses were now screaming with laughter.

I picked that moment to step inside the door. The cooks were still choking, tears running down their faces, but Pop stopped in mid-laugh and glared at me.

"Where'd you run to, boy?"

"I . . . uh . . . I . . . uh, just ran."

"Well, what're you doing sneaking into this kitchen?"

"I, uh . . . I thought maybe I could get some bread or something . . . " I mumbled.

"You got anything for him to eat?" Pop asked the cook.

"Supper's gone, but I could fix him a peanut butter and jelly sandwich and a glass of milk."

"Well . . . all right," Pop said. "Listen," he hissed at me, "you get done eating, you get back to the cabin pronto, you hear?"

"Yes, sir."

Pop's eyes had a glint in them, but it wasn't all malice. "And if Paul says anything to you, you tell him I beat the tar out of you . . . understand?"

"Yes, sir!"

Pop banged the screen door for emphasis as he left.

I took a big swig of milk and a huge bite out of the sandwich. I noticed that the cooks had put extra jelly on the peanut butter.

Sportsmanship and Channel Catfish

My education was enhanced in two important aspects during the summer of 1934, when I was age thirteen. The lessons were learned from two of the most skilled anglers I ever met—Bev Skaggs and Billy Warren. The learning was done on the same stretch of the same river, but in completely different disciplines. Bev was a fly-rodder, Billy a live-bait angler.

Bev Skaggs was the first real fly-fisherman I had met up to that time, a business college student some five years my senior, who had acquired his skills with the long rod from a friendly, elderly doctor he met by chance on the river. The doctor spent as many hours on the stream as he could spare from a busy practice, brief respites from the real and imaginary ills of humankind. Like many a young man in the Depression era, Bev had no money to invest in fishing tackle; but the good doctor had taken a liking to this quiet, studious young man and had provided an old but serviceable fly rod, plus a reel, line, and leaders, along with some patient schooling in the gentle art of laying out a fly with ease and precision.

Bev's family lived next door to my Aunt Lucille on Woodlawn Avenue in a quiet little town that consisted of an East Side and a

17

West Side, fortunately divided by a river that flowed through the middle. At that point in my life, fishing was my principal reason for existence, and it was with considerable excitement that I discovered the young man living next door to my aunt was considered one of the more skilled anglers on the entire West Side. The excitement was further heightened when he invited me to go along on one of his regular evening trips to the river, five blocks distant. My angling equipment at that time consisted of a somewhat bent tubular steel casting rod and an ancient casting reel, which my father had given me because the bearings were shot and it would no longer perform.

Let me hasten to explain that the river, at this midwest geographic location, was no pristine wilderness waterway. There was what could be called a segment of whitewater, the foaming spillway of a dam just upstream from the Galena Avenue Bridge, the concrete span that carried some of the city's busiest traffic. The dam and bridge were shaded by a tall hotel and the spire of the Paramount Theater. Indeed, it was quite common, when fishing near the bridge, to have evening theatergoers pause, lean on the bridge rail, and watch to see if there was any fishing activity before going inside to see the feature film. Below Galena Avenue, the river wound its way past the city library and post office, occasionally accepted outfall from a half dozen storm sewers, and passed beneath several other bridges, including one for rail traffic. It exited the downtown area at North Avenue, adjacent to the city gas plant, an impressive structure containing tall smokestacks, one of which continually belched forth a tall orange column of flame along with a pungent gassy aroma.

So much for the scenic aspects. The river, did, however, harbor a viable population of smallmouth bass, panfish, catfish, garfish, crawfish, turtles, muskrats, and other aquatic denizens. On our first foray, our targets were smallmouth bass and rock bass, which hung out in the riffles and behind the bridge piers adjacent to Hurd's Island, just across from the gas plant.

As we waded out into the current, upstream from the island, I confidently impaled a nightcrawler on my hook and let it drift downstream with the aid of a large cork bobber. Action was immediately forthcoming. The bobber bounced, then dove under, and I managed to crank in a stubby half-pound rock bass, and carefully placed it on a rope stringer. I had drawn first blood.

"Nice fish," Bev commented, raising my self-esteem a notch. But then he began to work out a long line, laying a tiny fly-and-spinner combination unerringly in the eddies curling around the North Avenue bridge piers, spots not within reach of my modest tackle. He promptly had a take from a foot-long smallmouth that put a fine arch into his bamboo rod and conducted a surface-breaking performance before being led out of the fast water and into a shoreline eddy for landing. Score: one apiece, and more on the way.

Somehow, my angling intensity began to fade with the day, and at sunset I found myself more fascinated with the mechanics of my companion's delivering small flies on a long line and fine leader. Eventually, I ceased fishing just to watch. At one point, Bev glanced up, motioned me over, and—wonder of wonders—handed me his rod. "Like to try it?"

Awkwardly self-conscious at holding such a light, responsive piece of angling equipment, I succeeded mainly in wrapping the line around my head in my disastrous first efforts. However, with some patient instruction and a little practice, I found I could retrieve the line off the water with a quick back cast, then whip the fragile stick forward, laying the line and fly in the general direction of the river. The casts were not neat, nor of any great distance, but I was fly-casting. I had joined the exalted ranks of angling's hierarchy!

As this revelation burst upon me, there was the certainty that nothing would deter me until I had my own fly-fishing outfit. A bobber with a nightcrawler suspended below might be sufficient to acquire the raw material for a fish dinner, but I sensed that casting a fly was a form of angling melding science with art.

Thus it was, upon returning home from this visit to Aunt Lucille's, that I immediately set about seeking the wherewithal to acquire my own fly-casting outfit. I saved nickels and dimes from my newspaper route, barbered countless lawns, pulled weeds, scoured back alleys for bottles that might have one- or two-cent deposit value at Riva's Grocery Store, and refrained from indulging in all of my usual vices, such as nickel steins of ice-cold A & W root beer and packs of Wrigley's Spearmint gum. At some point, I added up my horde and discovered I could afford a $3.69 bamboo rod at Montgomery Ward, plus a $1.15 single-action fly reel, a $1.25 enameled line, some leaders, and flies. I was in business. And I immediately headed on my bike for a nearby creek where, to my satisfaction, I caught several nine-inch bass on a streamer fly.

Seeking to expand my knowledge, I began to frequent the magazine rack at Doc Lenz's drugstore, where I devoured countless articles on fly-fishing presented in publications like *Hunting and Fishing, National Sportsman*, and *Field and Stream*. An absorption that was, unfortunately, sporadic, because Doc usually threw me out for reading and not buying. After a couple of weeks of study and practice, I felt ready for the major leagues. For one-half of my $1.50 weekly salary, I hired a substitute newspaper delivery boy, hopped on my bike with a small bag of clothing anchored to the handlebars and my fly rod lashed to the crossbar below the seat, and pedaled the eighteen miles over to Aunt Lucille's. When I headed for the river that evening with Bev, it was with a fair measure of confidence in my new-found piscatorial prowess and the opportunity to show it off.

It was that magical time of July when the descending sun converted the stream surface to a molten gold reflecting the upper stories of the hotel and the spire of the Paramount Theater. Traffic hummed on Galena Avenue, forming a duet with the cascade of water coming down the upstream dam. A hatch of insects, struggling to get off the water in the pool below the dam, were being systematically harvested by stubby rock bass, which, with scant discrimination, began scarfing up our flies with a considerable enthusiasm. Although I was aware that my casting skills were nowhere near as accomplished as my companion's, I managed to stay with him almost fish for fish. We each had eight nice panfish on our stringers as darkness approached, when suddenly Bev let out a grunt and arched his rod into something on a considerably more substantial scale. Where the water descending the dam spillway hit the pool below, an enormous smallmouth bass rocketed skyward and crashed back, leaped a second time with red gills flaring, then bored into the dark eddies. I stopped fishing to wade over and observe the battle, a furious joust with the bass alternately peeling off line, Bev fighting to get it back.

The contest ended ten minutes later in the shallows at the foot of the pool, where Bev reached down and lifted the tired warrior by its lower jaw, measured it against markings on his rod for a moment, muttered, "Eighteen and a half inches," then slipped the hook loose and lay the bass back in the water. Its fins fanned for a moment, then it flipped its broad tail and vanished into the pool.

I was dumbfounded. It was the largest smallmouth bass I had ever seen in the river up to that time. "Why'd you do that?" I yelled with a note of exasperation.

Bev smiled and looked me straight in the eyes: "I've got enough panfish for supper . . . besides, it would be a shame to kill a great fighter like that one."

Up to that time, I had never seen a fisherman let a large fish go free. Not my dad, not my uncle, nobody. Later that night, as I lay in bed, studying moths circling the streetlight outside the upstairs bedroom window, I pondered what had occurred. Somewhere in the confusion of my mind, I began to grasp the concept of sportsman-ship . . . that fishing might somehow be more than just hauling dead fish home to eat.

Two weeks later, I was back again, burning to tie into a big bass of my own. But Bev had determined that I needed to expand my horizons. "We're going catfishing with Billy Warren this evening," he announced.

Catfishing?

Up until the time I caught that first bass on a fly rod, catfish were a highly regarded species. Although not classified as game fish, they were strong fighters, would take almost any kind of bait, and were fairly numerous if one knew where to look. However, fly-rod fishing for bass had become my current obsession. Perhaps it had become time to obsess back to a less pretentious species. And who would be better to fish with than Billy Warren, a recognized catfish expert. According to Bev, the best. Billy lived with his mother and father in a modest frame house a block away from my aunt's. Quite often, we stopped on our way to the river, and Billy walked with us. And sometimes we walked home together. On those occasions, Billy's mother usually invited us in for cookies and glasses of cold milk.

On this particular evening, Billy had left for the river early, but his mother told us he would be fishing somewhere near the railroad bridge. In due course, we found him knee-deep in the current, a pair of fork-tailed, steely-blue channel catfish already on his stringer. He greeted us with a wide grin as we waded in alongside, but in-formed us that the catfish were not very active. What he said was: "The katefish ain't bitin' very good."

He always laughingly termed the species "katefish," sort of a private joke that we shared.

Our baits were chunks of Velveeta™ cheese, sometimes quite effective, but other than the first two on the stringer, the fish refused to cooperate. At length, Billy tipped back his battered felt hat, scratched his head, and said, "We jes' as well head home . . . the katefish sure enough quit for tonight."

Over milk and oatmeal cookies at Billy's house, we discussed the habits of our whiskered targets. "Maybe they're goin' better in the early mornin'," Billy offered. "And maybe on somethin' with a little more flavor."

"What would that be?" Bev asked.

Billy laughed. "I think I got jes' the thing cookin' up under a bridge pier . . . if you want to go tomorrow morning."

"What kind of bait are you talking about?"

"Clam meat. Got a two-pound coffee can of cut-up clam meat stuck up on a pier for the last three days . . . oughta be ripe by now. Meet you at six."

At five the next morning, Woodlawn Avenue was awakened by the sporadic clop-clop made on the brick pavement by the hooves of the milkman's horse. The sound stopped when the milkman hoarsely yelled, "Whoa," followed by the clink of milk bottles being deposited on back porches; then it resumed as the milkman made a clucking sound, sending the horse to the next cluster of houses.

By six, Bev and I were on the street, rods in hand. Billy, just finishing breakfast, came out with toast and jam in one hand, fishing tackle in the other. In the early morning sunlight, the city was awakening. Traffic sounds mingled with the slam of screen doors and the chirrup of robins as we walked down to the river.

Clams were familiar creatures to Billy, who spent much of his spare time harvesting the bivalves, wading hour after hour in the shoals, dragging a floating washtub. When the tub was full, the clams were transferred to gunny sacks and hauled home to be steamed open over a backyard fire. The shells were stacked until they could be hauled to a button factory downriver, where a ton brought thirty-two dollars. In a good week, Billy picked a half ton, providing much-needed cash to his Depression-strapped family. The clam meats were usually carried back to the river and dumped along the shore, to the delight of raccoons, gulls, and other scavengers. Except, in this instance, the ones Billy had cut into bait-sized pieces and stored in the coffee can.

"Whooee, these got power!" Billy announced as he retrieved the can from under the railroad bridge pier. "Ol' katefish gonna love these."

He hooked the can on his belt with a piece of wire as we waded into the current. At the bottom of a riffle, we each hooked a piece of rancid clam on a size two hook and drifted the bait downstream. Baiting up was not an easy task, considering the stench involved. The only way we could keep our eyes from watering and stomachs from churning was to hold the chunks of clam meat at arm's length downwind while impaling them on the hook. But Billy was right about the gustatory preferences of the whiskered fish population: catfish struck with unusual abandon. The bait would drift downstream, swirling and tumbling with the current, followed by the telltale thump of a strike and a swift run across current while we fed out slack. Tightening up, we hauled back and set our hooks into sleek, fork-tailed fighters from a pound to three pounds, just right for the frying pan. On my fly rod, the battles were intense, about equal to that of a bass, except the catfish, of course, did not provide any spectacular leaps.

It was close to noon when we climbed out of the river with all the catfish we could possibly haul home on three stringers. "Whooee . . . I bet some of these katefish come clear up from the Gulf of Mexico when they smelled that ol' clam meat," Billy laughed.

We hit one of the main streets for home but had to pause for a traffic light at an intersection in the middle of downtown. So did a lot of other people—clerks, stenographers, tradesmen, office managers—all on their way to lunch. While waiting for the light to change, some of the people began to crowd around to view our fish . . . but then, just as quickly, began to move away, coughing and looking somewhat ill.

Billy still had the coffee can of dead clams fastened to his belt, and Bev whispered: "I think we've got a pretty strong aroma about us . . . let's get moving."

As quickly as we could, we crossed the street, then took all the back alleys home. The problem was, we had been handling those dead clams so long, our olfactory sense had developed a measure of tolerance. We guessed there was still an odor, but it didn't seem nearly as strong as it did when we first started fishing.

I flipped my stringer of fish proudly up on Aunt Lucille's back porch and she came to view my catch. "Oh, what a nice bunch of . . . " She paused, looked sharply at me, and grabbed her nose. "Migod! What have you gotten into?"

"Clams," I said. "We were using dead clams for bait."

"Well, you just get those clothes off right away and get upstairs and into the bathtub . . . and you scrub until there isn't even a sug- gestion of clam on you. I'll have to run your clothes through the washing machine."

"What'll I do with my fish?"

"We'll worry about that later. Now, get!"

I got. I don't recall ever using rotten clam meat for bait again, no matter how effective it might be. But I did fish with Billy a number of times over the next two years. Occasionally, when I stopped by for him, he would be gone to the river already. "Billy sure loves that old river," his mother would say, shaking her head. "I guess he loves that old river because it's friendly . . . don't ever give him any trouble . . . don't make him feel bad."

I really didn't understand what she meant, not then. One day when I had come back from the river and had enjoyed milk and cookies at Billy's house, Aunt Lucille drew me into the kitchen with sort of an uncomfortable look and said, "Maybe you shouldn't hang out with Billy so much."

I was incensed. "Hey . . . Billy Warren is one of the best fishermen around . . . certainly the best catfish angler on the river."

"Well, I understand that," Aunt Lucille said with some embarrassment. "And it doesn't bother me, but some of the neighbors are talking about you spending so much time down at Billy's house."

"Well, sure. Billy's mom always has oatmeal cookies and milk for us when we come home . . . what the heck is wrong with that?"

"Nothing, really," Aunt Lucille replied, with that embarrassed look still on her face. "I don't mean you shouldn't go fishing with him, but maybe you could spend a little less time at his house."

This was baffling and I wondered about it; but Aunt Lucille never brought up the subject again.

As I grew up, the trips to my aunt's grew fewer, then ceased. In high school, I learned to drive and could then use the family Ford to reach any of the rivers in the area. By the time college beckoned, I had acquired an Old Town canoe, which opened up more angling vistas. And I was becoming aware of the somewhat flawed society in which we lived. I was in college when the war broke out, and it was a number of years before I got back to visit with Aunt Lucille, now living in a more upscale part of town. We reminisced about the old days, and she revealed that Bev had also returned from the service. I phoned my old fishing friend, and drove over for a visit. We talked and laughed about good times on the river, but things had changed during the war. Bev said fishing wasn't what it used to be. "Lots of pollution now . . . the fish are pretty well gone," he said, sadly.

"Remember the time you and I and Billy Warren got that big bunch of catfish on the rotten clams?"

"Yeah," Bev laughed shortly. "That was a long time ago."

"Does Billy still go after catfish?" I asked.

"No." Bev looked away. "Billy got out of school and couldn't find steady work anywhere. Went in the army for awhile, then got out. Stopped fishing when the river went sour." Bev ran a hand over his forehead. "Got to hanging out with a bad crowd and started drinking some. Billy got shot in a fight somewhere. He's dead."

There was a long silence. Of course, by then I well understood what Billy's mother had said those years before: "I guess he loves that old river because it's friendly... don't ever give him any trouble... don't make him feel bad."

Billy Warren was the first friend I ever had who was black.

The Chicken Thief

No matter how many firearms a hunter may collect over a lifetime, the one that is never forgotten is that first one. When my father placed his well-used Remington .22 in my hands, making it my very own, it was more than just a long-awaited inheritance; it was a rite of passage like my first pair of long pants. That my parents had determined I was old enough and trustworthy enough to own a firearm was an incredible vote of confidence. There had been a long period of training, of days afield when my father drilled into me the mechanics and responsibilities of shooting; but now, the rifle was mine . . . and, of course, that ownership had to be exercised.

Unfortunately, it was summertime and months away from any hunting season. But in the rural area where we lived, there were such prolific, nongame species as starlings, crows, and gophers, species universally classified as "varmints" by neighboring farmers. Armed with a box of .22 cartridges, purchased with a portion of my $1.50 weekly wage earned delivering newspapers, I set forth with all the confidence and anticipation of Meriwether Lewis heading out to explore the upper Missouri River.

Ernest Stettler's farm, which lay directly behind our home, was bisected by a small creek with shaded, tree-lined shores, an oasis of elms, box elders, and willows that wound behind a cluster of weathered barns and sheds. It was to that creek I repaired, rifle in hand, on that hot, dusty afternoon, seeking whatever adventure might ensue. On the swaying tip of a tall windswept elm, I spotted a pair of starlings raucously discussing the day's events. Hastily, I leveled off on the most visible bird, pulled the trigger . . . and missed. At the sound of the shot, the elderly landowner, of Swiss descent, came around the corner of the chicken house and called to me in his thick German accent:

"Hey, you! Hey you, Pob Cary! You pring dot rifle ofer here, quick, yah?" Somewhat apprehensive, I strode to the corner of the barnyard, expecting the old man to berate me for shooting too close to the buildings. Instead, he said: "Hey! Vee got a shicken t'ief in da henhouse . . . you vant to shoot a shicken t'ief vor me?"

"Chicken thief?"

"Yah . . . it vass dot shtinkin' raccoon vhat vas mine shickens shtealing . . . fife uff dem, already, yet."

Raccoon? This was an intriguing development, almost in the realm of big game hunting . . . certainly more exciting to a fourteen-year-old than starlings.

The old farmer brushed tobacco juice from his luxuriant mustache. "Yah . . . in da shicken house . . . come on, I vill you showing."

I followed the overall-clad figure as he shuffled through the barnyard, carefully sidestepping plops of cow manure. At the door of the henhouse, he placed a finger to his lips: "Shhh," he whispered. "Vee don' vant to shcare him."

Still uncertain as to what lay ahead, I leaned over to peer inside as he swung the rickety door open. A half dozen plump Plymouth rock pullets clucked and shuffled their feet on the roost, and the yeasty odor of straw mixed with chicken manure met my nostrils. But I didn't see any sign of a raccoon. "Where is it?" I whispered.

"Unter da floorpoards." He pointed downward, then drew me

back outside by the sleeve. "He vas shneakin' in all da time to shteal da shickens, und I shtuck a trap down unter a loose floorpoard."

"He's in a trap under the floorboards?"

"Yah," the old man nodded. "Dot's how he gets in . . . comes up t'rough a loose floorpoard.

"How do you know he's there?" I was not completely convinced.

"Because vhen I vas come to get da eggs, I hear dot raccoon shcrambling and shumping around down dere."

I peeked back inside the door. "Well . . . how the heck am I supposed to shoot it?"

The old man waggled a bony finger and winked. "Tell you vhat . . . I lift up da poard vere the raccoon iss, und you shoot, yah?"

"O.K.," I agreed, still somewhat skeptical that there was any live creature under the henhouse floor. Old man Stettler went to the hay barn to get a pitchfork, and I kept watch on the chicken house. The Plymouth rocks had gone back to sleep on the roost. A few blueflies buzzed over the chicken manure. There was no sound from under the floor.

The old man returned with the pitchfork. "You ready, ya?"

"Sure . . . I'm ready." I got the rifle to my shoulder, slipped off the safety button and lined in the sights. Stealthily, the farmer eased the tines of the fork under the loose floorboard as I leaned over, rifle muzzle aimed downward, and he lifted.

As the board came up, several things happened at once: Immediately, I saw the animal caught by a front leg in the steel trap. In that same split second my mind registered with horror that it wasn't a raccoon, but a huge and angry black-and-white skunk. We both fired point blank at the same time, while the chickens went squawking off the roost in a flurry of feathers.

I have no idea where my first shot went, but I know where his went. It hit me right in the face, blinding me with agonizing pain.

The Remington was a twelve-shot repeater, and I fired unseeing until the magazine clicked empty. Then I staggered backward, bounced off the door frame, and somehow lurched into the barnyard, where I gasped for air.

"Sheez!" The voice of the old farmer registered surprise. "Dot vas no raccoon . . . dot vas a shkunk!"

In my left hand I still gripped my rifle. With my right fist, I rubbed furiously at my burning, sightless eyes. "I'm blind!" I moaned, certain I was doomed to a life of begging on street corners.

"Vell, anyvay you finished dot shicken t'ief off . . . he is shtone dead already."

"Oh, God! I'm blind and maybe dying!" I wailed.

"No you chust got a liddle sqvuirt in your eyes . . . ve got to get your face vashed off . . . come on, ve go up py da horse tank." He grabbed my sleeve gingerly, as though to avoid any direct contact, and led me through a nightmare of eye-burning darkness.

Finally, we stopped. "Vait here," he ordered. "Here iss da horse tank . . . I vill go get a bucket to vash you off . . . " His footsteps retreated in the direction of the cow barn.

Reaching around, my hand came in contact with the worn, wooden side of the big, circular horse tank and I lay the rifle down. In desperation, I bent over and plunged my head into the cool water, sloshing my face back and forth, forcing my burning eyes open. At first nothing happened, but then I began to discern a sliver of light. More sloshing and the burning sensation began to subside; I could see more light. I pulled my head out, took a couple of deep breaths, and jammed it back into the water. After four treatments, I could begin to make out objects in the farmyard—the rusty steel frame of the windmill, the whitewashed concrete walls of the milk house, the farmhouse porch, the ramshackle toolshed, the cow barn.

Still gasping, I slid down with my back against the horse tank, tears streaming from my eyes, and tried to gather my wits. On the plus side, I was not totally blind, nor was I apparently in imminent danger of dying. On the minus side, I reeked.

At this exact moment, the farmer's wife came out of the kitchen door, a basket over her arm, heading for her vegetable garden. A thin, stooped, but wiry little woman with swept-back gray hair, she was always bubbling with friendliness.

"Hallo dere, Pob Cary . . . " she began, noticing the rifle. "Ernest said he vas going to get somebody to shoot dot raccoon vich vas coming to da henhouse . . . " At that point she got close enough for a good whiff of my fragrance.

"Oh, you bad poy!" she screamed. "You vas playing mit a shkunk!" She aimed a finger in the direction of our house across the distant fence line. "You get out uff here right now . . . you shtink, you bad poy . . . you shtink up da whole yard !"

Somehow, I got to my feet and managed to slink off, confused and humiliated. Here I had risked life and limb to save her lousy chickens and all I got was a face full of skunk juice and a lot of abuse. I don't know where the old man went . . . apparently, he couldn't find a pail.

Heading home, I crossed several fields and came in by the alley behind our garage to avoid any embarrassing confrontation with our neighbors. Crossing the backyard, I stopped below the screened kitchen window and peeked inside. I could see mom busy by the stove and I yelled through the screen: "Mom! Hey, mom!"

She came to the window. "What's wrong?"

"I got hit by a skunk," I said.

By that time a few strains of aroma had wafted through the screen. She recoiled and said: "Well, I guess! . . . Go farther out in the backyard and take off all your clothes . . . I'll fill the bathtub."

Somewhat self-conscious that the neighbors might be looking,

I peeled off my stench-drenched garments and dashed through the back door. Mom had the bathtub full of hot water, to which she had added a strong dash of ammonia.

"Get in!" she ordered, tossing a towel, washcloth, and bar of soap in my direction, then slammed the bathroom door shut.

The ammonia smarted my nose and eyes slightly, but nothing like what the skunk did. Whatever the chemical combination of ammonia and soap, it rendered me fairly human again. I emerged and dried off while the water gurgled down the drain. Mom cracked the door open and shoved fresh underwear inside.

With all the windows in the house open, whatever aroma had trailed in with me eventually seemed to dissipate. By the time my father came home from the office, the scent indoors was barely noticeable.

"Must have been a skunk went through the neighborhood," he observed as he came in the front door.

"The skunk was in the backyard," Mom said. "He left his clothes hanging on the bushes."

Pop went to the kitchen window and looked out. "What happened?"

"Well, Mr. Stettler asked me to shoot a raccoon that was sneaking into his henhouse . . . " and I went on to describe the whole story. Mom giggled, but Pop looked at me with considerable skepticism. I am sure he didn't believe a word I said.

But then, he never did, anyway.

The Great Pigeon Caper

It all started when Bob Spangler got the .410 single-action shotgun for his birthday, a year after my parents gave me the .22 caliber rifle. The rifle accounted for a couple of squirrels and rabbits that first fall, a somewhat rewarding circumstance from my standpoint since it not only moved me, at age sixteen, into the ranks of grown-up hunters, but it created a lot of satisfactory envy among my neighborhood peers, Spang and Jack Darkins.

The .22 rifle, however, paled in comparison to the .410 shotgun. Even though the .410 was the smallest smoothbore weapon made—discharging only a half ounce of bird shot when fired—it opened the possibility of shooting flying targets, something not possible with the rifle. Somehow Spang seemed adept in steering any conversation, even about the current baseball season, into the realm of fall hunting and what he would be doing in marsh and upland, wing shooting ducks, pheasants, and bobwhite. From what we could glean from reading outdoors magazines, wing shooting was the pinnacle of hunting sport.

Darkins was almost totally left out of the hunting picture. He had no weapon at all, and when hunting discussions came up, he either feigned disinterest or inquired if he could come with and maybe take a few shots himself. Things came to an abrupt head on a warm July day when we gathered in Spang's garage to consume a pair of ripe muskmelons we had just liberated surreptitiously from Mr. Barthleme's neighboring fruit and vegetable farm.

"My uncle Frank," Spang mumbled through a dripping mouthful of melon, "says he's got . . . about a million too many . . . pigeons at the farm . . . they're poopin' all over the hay . . . he wants to get rid of 'em."

Darkins and I looked up from our melon slices. "Yeah?"

"I'm figuring on going over to Frank's farm and shoot me a mess of pigeons tomorrow . . . kind of practice for next fall's duck season," Spang said.

We were well aware that every farm in the area had a thriving population of semiwild brown, gray, and white pigeons. A few farmers raised pigeons for squabs, which were sold to local restaurants, but most ignored the birds that simply hung out, fed on stray grain, and multiplied. However, this was the first indication we had that pigeons were dispensable, perhaps even a species to be hunted. "My pop said I could use the car . . . anybody want to go with?"

It was summertime, school was out, we were all sixteen years old, and there was not a whole lot going on outside of baseball on Saturday. "I'll go," I said. "I'll bring my .22."

Darkins looked doubtful. "I dunno," he said. "I don't have anything to shoot."

"Get some shells and you can shoot my .410."

"How about me?" I asked. "Can I shoot it, too?"

"Get your own shells."

At Barrett's Hardware Store, we knew that shells were a dollar for a box of twenty-five, or they could be purchased singly at five cents each. Spang had a full box his parents provided with the gun. Darkins and I immediately set out to acquire some .410 ammunition of our own. The opportunity to shoot at flying targets was something we simply could not pass up.

I had a quarter left from my weekly paper route. This was supplemented by scrounging up fifteen empty pop bottles from trash cans in neighborhood alleys. The one-cent-per-bottle deposit collected at Riva's Grocery boosted my net worth to forty cents, enough for eight shells. Darkins went into the lawn-cutting business for a day, barbering enough grass to purchase ten shells. Thus amply supplied, we embarked the following day in Spang's dad's Pontiac for the farm, some twelve miles to the east.

Naturally, we did not reveal the main goal of our expedition to our parents. We merely said we were going to Frank's farm to "help with the chores." We knew instinctively that any suggestion we were heading out with guns to wreak havoc on the pigeon population would have resulted in a firm "no!" Whatever birds we managed to bag, we decided, would become the entrees for an outdoor cookout at our clubhouse, a ramshackle edifice we had constructed of boards years earlier in a nearby field.

Our route from our rural homes led up a series of gravel roads and passed within a half mile of the state prison, a huge, concrete place of confinement surrounded by a high wall on which were posted guards armed with high-powered rifles. It was a barren, forbidding place, reportedly housing some of the nation's most desperate criminals. We drove past silently, staring at the walls and the tiny uniformed figures with guns. "Wouldn't want to be stuck in that place," Darkins noted as the prison dropped out of sight behind us.

Fifteen minutes later, we were in the farmyard being greeted by Spang's uncle Frank. "Shoot all the dang pigeons you want," he told us. "All they do is dirty up the hay." Then he noticed me taking the .22 rifle out of the car. "No, don't use that," he said. "I don't want no holes shot in the barn roof . . . you kids do all your shootin' with that .410 shotgun at the birds in the air."

I put the rifle back in the car, and we headed for the cow barn with Spang's .410 and our supply of ammunition.

Before we rounded the corner of the barn and saw the flock of birds roosting on the corrugated tin roof, we heard the "cluck-a-ta-coo, cluck-a-ta-coo" pigeon talk.

"I get first shot," Spang whispered tersely, eyeing the mob of sitting birds. "It's my shotgun."

"Dibs on second," I said quickly. Darkins shrugged, fingering the shells in his pocket and studying the colorful mass of birds. There must have been two hundred of them, many times more than the number of shells we possessed.

"Listen," Spang whispered. "I'll go around to the side and you guys hum a couple of rocks at the barn roof to make 'em fly. I'll blast into the flock as they go past." With that, he vanished around the side of the barn.

Darkins and I picked up some rocks and fired them at the tin roof. They hit the roof and banged along the corrugated tin. About half the pigeons woke up, flapped into the air, and swept around the corner. We heard a loud boom. Two more rocks got the rest of the startled birds airborne, and there was another boom. Darkins and I ran to view the carnage.

"How many did ya get?" I yelled.

Spang was standing silent, looking at the departing flock of pigeons, now a mass of dots winging over a distant pasture. "Well, how many'd you get?" Darkins asked, looking around.

Spang shook his head. "None."

"None?" We were dumbfounded. "How could you miss two mobs like that?" Darkins snorted in disbelief.

Spang shrugged.

"Well, it's my turn now," I confirmed. "I saw a bunch more pigeons in the toolshed. Boost 'em out and I'll nail 'em."

There were a couple of boards missing from the gable end on the south side of the toolshed, a means of entrance and exit for the birds. I shoved a shell into the .410 and stationed myself below the hole. "O.K., run 'em out!"

I heard Spang and Darkins hollering, "Shoo!" A half dozen pigeons shot out of the hole like rockets and flared upward. I swung at the bunch, pulled the trigger, and experienced a slight recoil as the gun went off. The pigeons kept on flying. "Some more comin'!" Spang called from inside. Four more pigeons swooped out, down, and then upward. My second shot was as futile as the first. Darkins ran out of the shed. "How many'd you get?"

I shook my head.

"Oh, for cryin' out loud!" He grabbed the shotgun out of my hands and stuffed a shell in the breech. "There are two more inside the shed. Run 'em out and I'll show you how it's done!"

I went back in the toolshed with Spang. The two pigeons were watching us nervously from a rafter in the back. We found some old rusty carriage bolts and hurled them at the birds. They both took off and flew through the hole in the gable end. "Pow!" went the .410. We ran outside. "Get 'em?" Spang yelled.

Darkins shook his head in complete embarrassment. Spang immediately took his shotgun back. "It looks like it is a lot harder to hit these doggone things than we thought," he observed. "Maybe we aren't swinging fast enough with the flocks or aren't giving them enough lead." In the outdoor magazines we had read all about "lead." This was computed as how far ahead of a flying target one should aim at any given range in order for the shot and birds to arrive at the same place at the same time. Since we had no experience at wing shooting, we didn't have much of an idea how this worked. But we still had a lot of shells, and our enthusiasm was not diminished.

Apparently our haphazard shooting did not particularly frighten the pigeons, because they kept circling around and coming back to the barnyard. We used the toolshed as a hiding place, stepping out to fire away at whatever flew past. Over two hours of dismal marksmanship, both Darkins and I ran out of ammunition and Spang went through a dozen shells out of his box of twenty-five. "We might as well quit," Darkins suggested.

Spang and I nodded in sorry agreement. As we headed for the car, Spang's uncle Frank came out of the barn. "Heard an lot of shootin'," he noted. "Must've shot a pile of 'em, eh?"

"Not too many," Spang answered truthfully.

It was about 3:30 in the afternoon. We rumbled down the gravel road toward home in the Pontiac, not saying much of anything. Suddenly, there began a loud, rising wail from the direction of the prison, a signal reserved for an extreme emergency. We were fast approaching a crossing where the prison entrance road bisected the one we were on. Ahead appeared a flurry of flashing red lights in steamers of dust as a number of squad cars converged on the crossing.

"Holy cow!" Darkins yelped from the back seat. "Somebody must've busted out!"

Spang recovered first. "Geez, the guns! Duck the guns and shells!" he called over his shoulder at Darkins. In a flurry of action, Darkins jammed the shells down a crack in the upholstery and pulled a dusty car robe over the guns lying on the car floor. It was obvious we were too close to the roadblock to turn around in the middle of the road and head back the other way. And we were well aware that if the police spotted the guns we might be involved in a lot of unneeded trouble.

At the intersection, three state patrol cars were parked, engines running, red lights revolving. A half dozen officers in brown uniforms and peaked hats were on the road. One stood in the middle with one hand up, the other on his holster, flagging us to stop. Spang braked slowly and we stopped. The officer walked over and looked in the driver's side. "Where you kids going?" he asked, his eyes darting around the car interior.

"Going home," Span said, politely.

"Where's home?"

"Over there about six miles," Spang pointed.

He seemed satisfied, but a second cop had glanced in the back window. "Whatta you got here?" he barked, leaning down and jerking the robe off the two guns.

With that, all friendliness vanished. I found myself staring down the barrel of the largest revolver I had ever seen. Spang and Darkins were likewise on the wrong end of handguns. "Out! Out!" the cops yelled. "Get your hands high!"

We stumbled out and were jerked around to face the car. "Hands on top! Spread 'em!"

We had seen enough movies to know the routine. Legs apart, we leaned our hands on the car top while they patted us down.

"O.K., wise guys," the first cop said. "What're the guns for?"

"They're only a .410 and a .22 . . . we were pigeon hunting."

"Oh yeah? Where?"

"Over at my uncle Frank's farm." Spang struggled to keep his voice low and even, but it cracked a little.

"Where's Uncle Frank's farm?" the cop snarled derisively.

Spang a moved a hand to point back the way we had come, but the cop jammed a revolver against his ear. "Don't get cute, kid," he hissed.

One of the cops was on his squad car radio. " McNally in car twelve," he said. "Picked up three guys with two guns."

There was some crackling on the radio and talk from the other end we couldn't hear.

"Yeah . . . in a nineteen-thirty-five blue Pontiac . . . Illinois license three-twenty-seven, four-four-six."

There was some more crackling on the radio. "Request we bring 'em in," said the cop named McNally. "Hold 'em until we find out what this is all about."

There were some more garbled words. McNally turned to two other cops. "Take 'em to the front office until the emergency is over and we can sort this out."

One of the other cops barked at Spang. "Where's your friend hiding?"

"What friend? This is all of us," Spang said in a quavering voice.

"Ah, come on, kid. You were gonna meet your friend out here with the car and guns and help him get away, right?"

A cold finger of fear ran down my spine. Spang was white as a sheet. But Darkins, who always was the most gutsy of our gang came firing back: "Hey . . . if we were out to help break some con loose, do you think we'd be using a little ol' .410 shotgun and a .22 rif . . . ."

"SHADDUP!" the cop screamed, waving his revolver. "And keep those hands on the car!"

"I don't like the looks of these kids," another cop said.

"Run 'em over to the office and lock 'em up for now, anyway," McNally told them.

At gunpoint, hands in the air, we were escorted to a squad car. We roared off in a cloud of dust, siren screeching, red light flashing. At the front gate of the prison, we were ordered out and marched up the steps and through two barred doors, which opened, then clanged shut behind us. In front of us was a desk with a beefy, red-faced sergeant. He speared us with slitted eyes. "Put 'em in the holding pen for trustees," he ordered.

We were ushered through another door with iron bars into a room with concrete walls. The door clanged shut. Outside of some wooden benches around the walls, there was nothing in the room except two convicts in faded blue overalls, swabbing the floor with mops. They immediately stopped and greeted us.

"Whatcha in for, bo?" the oldest one, with gray hair and faded eyes, inquired.

"Well, we got picked up with these two guns . . . " Darkins started to say.

"Hey!" the old con broke in. "Don't mess with no guns! Listen, guns is what got me in here. Got one year left to serve on a manslaughter rap. See, I caught my wife messin' with another guy an' I trailed 'em to a party and shot at the guy through a window. Missed him . . . but hit another guy by accident. Killed him dead." He spit on the floor and ran the mop over it. "Got a one-to-ten for manslaughter, that's what I got."

"Yeah, but we didn't do anything," Spang said.

Both convicts hooted uproariously at this. "Hey, ain't nobody in this place ever done nothing," the old one said and resumed pushing his mop, chuckling.

We sat down on one of the wooden benches and tried to gather our wits.

"They can't keep us in here," Darkins whispered. "We aren't charged with anything."

"If you hadn't done such a lousy job of hiding the guns we wouldn't be here at all," Spang growled.

"What time is it?" I asked.

Spang had the only watch. He glanced at it. "Quarter to five."

"Geez, if I'm not home by suppertime, I'm gonna be in a lot of trouble," I said.

Both of the convicts cracked up at that one. "If he ain't home by suppertime! Haw! Haw! Haw!" The younger one wiped tears from his eyes.

I walked over to the barred door and peered out into the office.

"Look!" I called to the desk sergeant. "I got to call home and tell my mother where I am or she's gonna be sore."

"SHADDUP!" the desk sergeant yelled back. The two convicts doubled up with laughter again.

"You shut up, too," the red-faced cop yelled.

I sat back down on the bench. Five o'clock was suppertime at our house. My mom, dad, and sister would be sitting down and my whereabouts would be severely in question. Absence at dinnertime at our house was a capital offence.

I went back to the bars. "Hey, honest," I pleaded. "I got to call home."

"SHADDUP!!"

The two front doors clanged and some officers came in. They glanced at us with curiosity. "The kid there says he's got to call home," the sergeant said to one the officers, obviously in charge.

The officer, a flinty-eyed veteran, came over and sized me up. "Where's home, kid?" he asked.

"About six miles west," I said. "It's suppertime and my mom and dad are gonna be furious. My dad is liable to kill me."

"What's your name?"

"Cary . . . Bob Cary."

"Yeah? Who's your dad?"

"Rex Cary." Fortunately Rex was not an ordinary name. It was one easily recognized in our small town.

"Rex Cary your dad?"

"Yes, sir!"

"What's your phone number?"

I told him. He went over and picked a phone off the desk, telling the operator the number. Apparently my mother answered right away because he said: "Mrs. Cary? This is Captain McKnight at the state prison . . . do you have a son Bob? Uh-huh. You do? Uh-huh. Well, we have him locked up over here . . . ."

This apparently occasioned a gale of laughter from my mother.

"McKnight. Yes, I'm Captain McKnight." He turned to the beefy sergeant. "She doesn't believe me."

"Yes, Mrs. Cary," he continued, "I'm sure your son is a good boy and never did anything wrong, but we have him locked up over here . . . "

He paused again, listening to my mother. "No, I am not kidding. See, we had a prison break today, and he got picked up with two other boys . . . sure . . . well . . . is Mr. Cary home? Uh-huh . . . could I speak with him?"

There was a pause, then: "Hello, Rex. This is Captain McKnight over at the state prison . . . fine . . . hope you are too . . . Say, we had a breakout here today, and we picked up your boy and two others driving by in back . . . Yeah . . . They had a couple of guns in the car . . . Yeah . . . I'm at the front gate . . . I'll be looking for you."

He hung up.

"He's coming over," McKnight said.

I didn't know if this was good or bad. It was scary enough to be behind bars, but I was really worried about what my dad was liable to do. I didn't think the cops would kill me, but I wasn't sure about my father.

Fifteen minutes went by, and the two doors clanged again. In came Pop, fire in his eyes. "O.K., what'd they do?" Pop said.

Captain McKnight laughed. "Probably nothing. These kids said they were hunting pigeons with a rifle and a shotgun and were on their way home when our alarm went off. They ran into three of our squads at the crossroads. Understandably, our men were jittery with the convict running loose and these kids with guns . . . "

"Sure." Pop seemed to cool down just a few degrees. "But they really didn't do anything?"

" No . . . if you sign for 'em, we'll let 'em go. And we've got their car in the yard. One of 'em can drive it home."

Pop went over to the desk and signed a paper. The sergeant unlocked the door.

"Hisst!" The older convict gave me a look. "Glad you're gettin' out, kid. Your dad a lawyer?"

"Nope," I said with real sincerity, "but thanks."

We went out through the two clanging doors. I took a deep breath. Never had the grass looked greener, the sky bluer.

Spang said, "Thanks Mr. Cary," sprinted over to his dad's car, revved it up, and drove out quickly.

On the way home, we filled Dad in with most of the details of the day, only omitting any we thought might incur his wrath. Dad let Darkins off at his house and then drove me home to supper. Mom's eyes were big as saucers as I told my story, including our discussion with the two convicts, embellishing it all with considerable bravado.

"All the time I thought it was one of your father's friends on the phone trying to pull a trick on me," she said. "My word, you really were in the prison."

"Yeah," I said, "but they couldn't scare us. We knew they couldn't hold us."

The next evening the story appeared in our daily newspaper. Bold, black headlines on the front page screamed, "POLICE DRAGNET NABS PIGEON HUNTERS."

They had our names and everything in the story, only the way it came out, the police said they locked us up because they were afraid the escaped convict might get his hands on our guns or the car. Anyway, for the next couple of days we were pretty hot stuff in the neighborhood. Everybody wanted to hear our story firsthand, and we told it, with a few added details here and there. But after a couple of days, it was old news and nobody wanted to hear it anymore.

Fame, we began to realize, was fleeting. When Spang, Darkins,

and I got together we figured John Dillinger probably kept robbing banks because if he didn't nobody would remember him.

"One thing," Darkins bragged, "none of those cops waving their guns in my face scared me a bit."

"Me, neither," said Spang.

"Me, neither," I lied, right along with them.

The Winchester Fly Rod

Just about everyone identifies Winchester as a maker of fine fire-arms—even individuals who never got any closer to a gun than watching a John Wayne western. But few people are aware that once, long ago, there was a Winchester brand of split bamboo fly rods, superb examples of the rod craftsman's art. One of these came into my possession during my sophomore year in high school, which happened to be 1937.

The rod came to me by way of Roy Nord, head of the sporting goods department in the biggest hardware store in my home town. No one ever handled a long rod with more skill and finesse than Roy, fifteen years older than me, who developed his proficiency on the crystal, cold trout streams of Upper Michigan, but who had migrated to my hometown when offered better economic opportu-nities for a young married man with a family on the way. Where I grew up, there were no trout. There were, however, a goodly num-ber of meandering smallmouth bass streams, which both Roy and I explored with diligence.

Like many masters of the tapered line, Roy preferred to fish quietly and alone. But he was not adverse to talking at length about fishing when some eager neophyte stopped in the sports depart-ment to fondle the finer rods or admire the exquisite products of the fly tier's vise. His house was on my newspaper route, and during the warm months, he would often be out on the front porch when I passed papers, and we would swap fishing stories for a few moments. One July evening, we did go fishing together in the Fox River, one of our better bass streams, one that also contained some stubby rock bass and long, fork-tailed channel catfish. For Roy, it was a relaxing evening plying the riffles and pools with his eight-foot Heddon rod, laying out line with grace and precision. For me, it was a learning experience. No matter how valiantly I tried with my heavy, bargain-basement tackle, it was readily apparent that I was greatly outclassed by Roy's talents. Effortlessly, he placed the fly on the very lip of an eddy, the exact edge of grass hanging from an undercut bank, or he roll-cast his offering deep into the shadows of overhanging willow boughs.

At length, I stopped casting altogether and just watched a master perform. Over an hour, Roy picked off a trio of thirteen-inchers, each of which was eventually swept up in a wood-frame landing net and released. As the sun faded and darkness moved in, we waded out of the river and shuffled up to Roy's car, where we took off our hip boots before stowing our tackle. Roy reached for my cheap rod, flexed it, shook his head, and solemnly handed it back.

"It's the best I can do on my paper route," I said, lamely.

Roy nodded. We got in his car and drove silently home.

A week later, Roy was sitting on his front steps as I came by with the newspaper. "If you've got a few minutes after you're through with your route, stop over," he said. Twenty minutes later I was back, and we filed into the living room. Roy's wife brought us each a cold bottle of root beer as we settled into soft chairs. I was busting to talk fishing, but somehow managed to politely keep my mouth shut. A lanky English setter strolled in and stretched out at Roy's feet.

After a long sip of root beer, Roy looked at me steadily for a moment, then leaned over and picked a four-foot cloth case from the floor beside his chair. "Open it up," he said, handing it to me with a faint smile.

"What is it?"

"Take it out and see. It's yours."

I untied the strings and tipped the case upside down. Three beautiful sections of bamboo fly rod appeared. With shaking fingers, I assembled the butt to the center section, center section to the tip. It was a fragile wand, extremely light and willowy, dark brown with bright gray-and-black silk windings. I ran my hands over the satin finish, then noted the familiar Winchester signature.

"I didn't know there was a Winchester fly rod."

"Not a lot of them," Roy noted. "But the ones that were made were top-notch."

"You're giving me this?"

Roy laughed. "I couldn't stand watching you flail around out there on the river with that crude outfit you were using." He took another sip of root beer. "I don't use this old rod any more . . . you just as well may have it. It's eight feet long, four ounces in weight, and casts like a dream . . . only it's very light and very soft. It won't handle anything heavy like spinners or cork bugs, but it's excellent for wet flies or streamers. And don't try to horse any fish in . . . won't take it."

I stammered thanks, finished my root beer, and peddled my bike like crazy for home in a rush to show my parents my good fortune.

From that point on, my angling success took a sharp turn for the better. The following Saturday, on the nearby DuPage River, I landed a brace of bass on a Reuben Wood streamer: one was a jut-jawed fifteen-incher that put an incredible arch in that willowy stick. When not in use, the rod was cased and stored over the mirror in my bedroom. Occasionally I took it down to run a cloth lightly over the smooth finish and read again "Winchester." It was the utter envy of

53

my angling peers, Spang and Darkins, who worked twice as hard at casting inferior equipment, with relatively meager results. Through winter, I dreamed of being on one river or other—a considerable amount of such dreaming unfortunately occurring during various school classes, much to the irritation of my teachers, who struggled mightily but futilely to supplant thoughts of bass fishing with theories of economics, algebraic equations, and the causes of the War of 1812. Several times, as I stared out the classroom window at the snow-blanketed school yard, my imagination swept me to one of the foaming rapids on the Kankakee River, and I recalled in exact detail just how the current swirled around a certain limestone ledge and swept past a clump of low-hanging willows. Invariably I would be jolted out of my reverie by an ill-timed and only half-heard question from the teacher, who, to my embarrassment and the hilarity of my classmates, had to repeat the inquiry. Such incidents resulted in several notes to my mother suggesting she have my hearing tested clinically.

But ever so slowly, as it does when one is a high school sophomore, June came around with accompanying warm weather, school dismissal, and Saturday ventures to the rivers.

My skills became more proficient, and I found I could lay a fly with almost as much delicacy as I had observed in Roy. Not as long a line, for certain, but with sufficient accuracy. And that was the summer I saw THE BASS.

The largest pool in my favorite stretch of the Fox River was perhaps forty yards long and five feet deep, with a huge boulder just below the surface at the deepest point. There were riffles at the head and tail of the pool, usually quite productive spots in hot weather when the stream was low and clear. It was a late June evening, and I had hit a pair of foot-long bass on a red-and-yellow Mickey Finn streamer in the lower riffle. I was wading round the deep water toward the upper riffle when I detected a shadowlike movement alongside the big boulder. Edging within casting distance, I lengthened the line with several false casts, then fired the streamer directly upstream from the rock. As it drifted down, I stripped line to give it an erratic, minnowlike movement. What looked like a piece of the boulder detached itself. Startled, I made out the shape of the largest bass I had ever seen, perhaps twenty-two inches in length. Five or six pounds!

He rose slowly to within inches of the drifting streamer, then just as slowly sank from view. A gasp of air shot into my lungs, and I realized I had been holding my breath through the entire episode. Recalling some of the lore absorbed from reading Dr. Roy Henshall, Ray Berglund, and other angling authorities, I quickly changed flies, tying on a coachman streamer with a white-hair wing. This done, I made several false casts and let the Winchester rod lay the coachman ever so lightly out and beyond the boulder. Again, I held my breath as the fly approached the lair and once more that mammoth brown form rose, and then vanished. A half dozen more casts brought no sign of him. But he was there, somewhere. An incredible trophy!

I cautiously skirted the balance of the pool and waded to the upper riffle, pondering what further course of action to take. Perhaps give him a half hour rest and come back for another try? It was getting late and might be too dark.

It was then I spotted the crawfish. The crawfish was about four inches long, in very shallow water, molting its hard outer coat, as crawfish do when feeding heavily and growing. An apparently plausible thought flashed through my head. As any fisherman knows, the preferred natural food of smallmouth bass is the crawfish. Particularly crawfish like this one, which after shedding its hard outer coat would remain in a soft-shelled, rubbery state for several hours until the new shell could harden. Thoughtfully, I plucked the unfortunate crustacean from the water, gently removed the remains of the hard shell, and went over to sit on a rock, changing my streamer fly for a regular size-two bait hook. I impaled the crawfish through the tail section so it would appear to be swimming naturally backward, then waded out, determined to ambush that monster smallmouth. I knew my light fly rod could not cast this weight, so I eased into a position some distance upstream from the big boulder and simply drifted the crawfish straight into the old monster's lair. For several seconds nothing occurred. Had he moved? Had my downstream approach spooked him?

Hah! I felt a light tug, quickly supplanted by a steady, powerful pull as the line stripped out in a rush. Hastily, I fed more slack, careful not to allow any tension. Far enough, I thought. Deadly intent, I stopped feeding slack and watched the line straighten out. When I felt a solid weight, I whispered, "Now!" I hauled back with a vengeance to drive the hook home and heard a loud, sickening "Crraack!" The entire forward section of the rod snapped off.

Realization first struck me that I should never have set the hook so hard with such a light piece of equipment. Secondly, I probably never should have gotten so excessively greedy and put that abominable crawfish on the line anyway. But, thirdly, as I stood there traumatized, with only the rod handle and reel, I became aware that there was still something out there on the end of the line. The fish was still on, cutting a long, powerful curve upstream. With my now abruptly shortened equipment, I set about grimly to the task of playing the trophy, feeling a glimmer of hope that if I could land that six-pound smallmouth bass, the disaster of the broken rod might somehow be offset. Indeed, I began to formulate a story to explain how this massive trophy tore up my fragile rod before I managed to capture it with an heroic effort. Perhaps, I mused, my father would have the big bass mounted by a taxidermist, and I could hang the shattered rod over it like the broken spear of a knight errant.

Using extreme care not to break the leader or tear out the hook,

I played the fish directly from the reel, taking in line furiously when he ran at me, letting it peel out when he ran the other way. After what seemed a lifetime, the great fish began to weaken. His rushes grew shorter, and he paused periodically to shake his head doggedly. Still, I hadn't glimpsed his thick, tan body, but there was plenty of time for that when the battle was won. Gently I worked him toward the downstream riffle and to an adjacent gravel bar. He came along sullenly, still fighting back. The last fifteen feet I coaxed both him and the broken piece of rod still hanging on the line around some rocks and then slid the whole works up on the bar, where the huge fish lay half in and half out of the water. Six pounds of gleaming, thrashing . . . catfish!

Disbelief flooded my mind. I stood stunned, staring at that long, bluish form, gills gasping spasmodically, rubbery whiskers drooping from his face.

Catfish? Never had I thought that the fish on the other end of the line could be anything but that huge bass. Migod, I had broken that beloved, wonderful Winchester rod on nothing but an ugly catfish!

Let me hasten to explain that under other circumstances, I would have been quite happy to land such a fish and would have taken it proudly home for mom to render into crisp, cracker-breaded fillets. But not at this time and place. For a full minute I just stood there in total dejection.

A golden sun was sliding into the tree-line willows. The evening mosquito horde was just beginning to hum, and great blue herons flapped past overhead with hoarse squawks. But none of this mattered. With resignation, I reached down and slipped the hook from that repugnant, whiskered face, put my toe against the middle of the catfish, and gave it a healthy push into the current.

At heart, I knew the catfish was not at fault. All the fault was mine: first, for trying to take that granddaddy bass with so under-handed a method; second, for doing such a dumb thing with such light tackle; and third, for allowing my imagination to deny the fact that there could be anything else in that pool except that one big bass. The bamboo fly rod was obviously not repairable. Sadly, I put the pieces back in the cloth bag, tied the strings, and headed home.

I had a shelf over the mirror in my room where I kept that broken rod for years afterward. I thought of throwing it out or burn-ing it, but I just couldn't. A number of times over the months after-ward, when I was in the hardware store, Roy would ask how the Winchester rod was working out. "Finest rod I have ever handled," I answered truthfully.

"Just don't try catching anything heavy on it," Roy would cau-tion. And I would wince with guilt.

By 1941, I had acquired two other rods, one a fine, lightweight Heddon model, about as close to the Winchester as I had been able to find. I was working, making pretty good money in a defense plant, saving up to complete my last two years of college, when the Japanese attacked Pearl Harbor.

A few weeks later, when I was packing up and leaving for the Marine Corps, Mom choked back a tear and said she was going to repaint my room and put up new curtains so it would look nice when I got back.

"What do you want me to do with a lot of that old stuff you've got up there?" she asked.

"Sort it out, save the good stuff, and throw out the junk."

"What about that fishing rod in the cloth case over the mirror?"

"It's broke," I said.

"It is? Why are you keeping it?"

"I don't know, Mom. I just couldn't throw it away."

I thought about that rod just once during the war. It was on the deck of an LST as we made ready for the assault on the Japanese island of Saipan. The largest task force in naval history lay offshore, hammering the enemy with thousands of shells, while dive bombers screamed over the island, unloading tons of bombs. With one of my squad, I leaned against the rail watching the carnage, fully aware that we would be in the middle of it within minutes.

"You know what today—June 15—is back home?" I asked.

"No." My Marine buddy looked at me sideways.

"It's opening day of the 1944 bass season, that's what. And I wish I was there."

"I wish I was there with you," my buddy said softly.

When I came home from the war, my bedroom had a new coat of paint, new curtains, and a new bedspread. The cloth bag with the Winchester rod was gone from over the mirror. "Guess she finally threw it out," I thought.

I opened my duffle bag and removed some khaki shirts and pants, which I carried to the closet to hang up. And then I saw it. Leaning in a corner of the closet was the old cloth bag. I took it out, sat down on the bed, untied the strings, and dumped out the bamboo sections. I ran my hand across the smooth varnish, inspected the piece that was fractured, and thought back to the big bass in the pool.

"I wonder if he is still there?" I said, half aloud. The war was finally over.

A Faint Odor of Fish

G. A., one of my early cohorts in seeking various wild creatures—feathered, furred, or finned—was considered variously by our high school peers as ornery, treacherous, and even devilish. Such appellations, I felt, were somewhat exaggerated. To me, G. A. was rather a person with a single-minded approach to life. That is, single-minded in the respect that his success came first, such details as fair play, good sportsmanship, and other encumbering details notwithstanding. Coupled with this was a somewhat devious mentality, which seemed to derive considerable pleasure from the discomfort of others. Outside of that, he was a heck of a fine friend. In addition, he had access to transportation—his father's Buick sedan.

On a particular fall day we were angling for crappies—gleaming, silver-sided, pie-plate-size panfish. It was that period of limbo between the end of serious summer bass fishing and the opening of the duck season. Indeed, the area where we pursued crappies was a shallow, weedy, stump-filled river backwater where we spent the majority of our duck-hunting time in pursuit of teal, mallards, wood ducks, and pintails. This last fling at open-water fishing had the secondary purpose of providing us with information concerning the current waterfowl population, feeding, and flight patterns. Thus, while pursuing crappies, we were also formulating plans as to where successful waterfowl ambushes might best be situated.

Wading in hip boots, we were each armed with bamboo fly rods and had each attached to our belts, by cords, floating tin buckets filled with shimmering shiners. Our terminal tackle consisted of six-foot leaders, small bobbers, and size-eight long-shanked hooks attached to No. 1 nickel spinners. In the somewhat murky backwaters, the flickering spinners seemed to add a decisive attraction to the bait.

Wading carefully in the icy water, we edged our way around stumps, logs, cattail clumps, and the occasional beaver house, working our baits close to the various structures where crappies might be lying in wait. The spinners were kept moving, both up and down and sideways, with frequent pauses. When the bobber stopped, then edged downward, we would wait for a few seconds, tighten up until the fly rod tip bent slightly, then set the hook with a firm lifting motion. Every few minutes, either G. A. or I would lift, sense a satisfying surge below the surface, and announce, "Got 'im!"

As the day wore on we had a fair number of "got 'ims" impaled on rope stringers attached to our belts. When the chill of evening began to numb our fingers and shivers started where the ice water pressed cold rubber against our shinbones, we reluctantly called it a day and awkwardly thumped in our boots back to the Buick.

This is where the trouble started, although it was not apparent to me at the time. We carefully laid our respective stringers of fish on an old newspaper in the car trunk, disjointed our rods, and exchanged the boots for shoes. While I was sitting on the Buick running board, tying my shoes, G. A. magnanimously offered to empty the minnows from my bucket, along with his, into the river since it was our last angling venture of the fall. Being absorbed with my shoelaces and not entirely alert, I said yes.

In a moment, G. A. returned, made a big scene of stowing the empty buckets in the trunk, and slammed down the lid. We got in the car and rode homeward, savoring the warmth from eight cylinders processed through the car's heater. En route, we discussed the coming duck season, laid plans accordingly, and guessed as to when the main flight would come down.

Opening day, at 4 A.M., I was assembling my hunting gear in the basement—Model 97 Winchester 12-gauge, a patched, hand-me-down canvas jacket with a black rubber Olt duck call in the upper left pocket, canvas cap, a half box of shells, a gunny sack full of solid cedar decoys, which over the years had acquired countless coats of dull enamel arranged, more or less, to resemble the plumage of drake and hen mallards. Also included were a lunch bag, thermos, license and duck stamp, and my hip boots.

I had been dimly aware over the past weeks that my mother was complaining that "something is dead" in the basement and urging me to search for what we assumed was a defunct mouse lodged in some out-of-the-way trap. On several occasions, I had searched behind the furnace, under the stairs, and among shelves of preserves; and while I, too, could detect the distinct aroma of death, nary a mouse turned up.

With the thermos stowed in the game pocket of my coat, shells inserted into the loops along the front pockets, I took my waders down from the hooks where they hung and jammed my stocking foot into the right boot leg. There was a sort of a squishing sound, and a near-overpowering stench gushed forth, indicating the source of the aroma that had permeated the basement. By the time I jerked my foot back out, the foul smell was bringing tears to my eyes and threatened to dislodge my breakfast. Had it been a rodent, as originally suspected, it would have had to have been the size of a beaver to create such a smell. Eventually, as my eyes cleared and I could inspect my sodden right sock, I recognized a mass of glittering scales and bits of fins. Obviously, G. A., in a fit of perversity, had deposited the leftover crappie minnows into my boot instead of the river.

As I was gagging and dabbing away at the mess with paper towels, the insistent honking of a car horn indicated G. A. had arrived in his dad's Buick. Realizing that any thorough effort would require a scrubbing out with laundry bleach, I simply jammed my boots on, shouldered my gun and decoys, and went out in the predawn darkness.

All day in the duck blind, when I had occasion to shift around on the hard board seat, a faint essence of dead shiner drifted up to my nostrils. I had no way of knowing if G. A. detected any untoward odor, because he made no mention. Neither did I. Indeed, he had recently received a neatly tailored L.L. Bean hunting jacket for his birthday, a fact he dwelt on at some length.

For an opening day it was not spectacular, but respectable. We managed a quartet of blue-winged teal, a drake mallard, and a somewhat wizened and poorly feathered hen bluebill. However, for two high school lads it was a fair measure of success. We parted company in high spirits, the condition of my boot interiors notwithstanding.

That night, after my three ducks were plucked, I worked diligently for two hours scrubbing out the boot liners with water, soap, and bleach, eventually restoring their interiors to the more acceptable and traditional smells of canvas and rubber. Nor did I tell my mother what had occurred, other than to say, "I found the dead mouse." My father had taught me early in life that real men not only don't cry, they coolly accept the unexpected barbs of fate hurled by insensitive humanity, but immediately seek an opportunity to retaliate. Christian forgiveness was deemed a worthy trait, but only after one had gotten even.

The duck season slid into the rabbit and pheasant seasons, and then it all ended. By mid-December, snow layered the fields. Lakes, ponds, and backwaters had a three-inch ice cover.

"Do you suppose the crappies would be feeding under the ice?" G. A. ventured one noon as we sat in the high school lunchroom stuffing down our peanut butter and jelly sandwiches.

"We'll never know unless we go," I countered.

The following Saturday we pooled resources, bought two gallons of gas at sixteen cents per, acquired two dozen shiners at Ace Bait for a quarter, bundled up in long johns, wool pants, and shirts, put extra sweaters under our canvas hunting coats, and headed for the backwaters, where we chipped in several holes with a hand ax. It took some time for the crappies to find us, but eventually, before we ran out of bait, we landed twelve nice panfish about a pound each, enough for fish fries at our respective homes. It was near dark when G. A. let me off in front of my house, leaning on the steering wheel while I jumped out and retrieved my tackle and fish from the trunk of the Buick. I paused, momentarily, noting that G. A. had stuffed his L.L. Bean hunting coat in the trunk on top of his gear. With a flourish I slipped two of my larger crappies through the side slit into the game pocket of his coat, slammed down the trunk lid, and bade my companion good night.

The following Wednesday, just before classes were to start, a red-faced G. A. braced me in front of the high school library. "You skunk!" he hissed, eyes glittering.

"What?" I feigned surprise.

"You lousy skunk. You dropped two crappies in the back of my new L.L. Bean hunting jacket."

"Me?"

"Yeah, you. I hung my jacket in the hall closet when I got home last Saturday, and by Tuesday when I was in school, my mother smelled it all the way in the living room. She opened the closet door and stuck her hand in the back of the jacket and it came out all covered with fish goo and crappie scales. She hadda take a sedative and go to bed. Now they got me grounded and I can't use the car for the New Year's Eve dance!"

"What makes you think I did it?"

"Who else coulda stuck those crappies in the jacket?"

"I dunno," I said. "Maybe the same guy who stuck the dead minnows in my boot."

G. A. stared at me, realization finally dawning.

"Tell you what," I said, forgiveness and magnanimity oozing through my veins. "I'll get my old man's Chevy and you can double date with my gal and me on New Year's."

There were some things in life, I found, about which my father was dead right.

Simply Shocking Fish Stories

Pale, blue-gray mist hung over the silvery surface of the DuPage River as B. J. Skaggs and I slid under the barbed wire cattle fence and stalked across the dew-drenched bluegrass pasture. It was one of those "Thank God I'm alive" mornings, with Canada thistles unfurling their purple heads, meadowlarks whistling cheery welcomes from cedar fence posts, and crows cawing raucously from distant woodlands.

A forever restless farm stream, clear and cool as well water, the DuPage each day added its flow to the headwaters of the Mississippi River, urgently, inexorably heading for the Gulf of Mexico some two thousand miles distant. Sometimes whispering over rocky riffles, sometimes curling beneath undercut, tree-shaded banks, it meandered almost imperceptibly through lily-lined pools where myriad crawfish furtively hidden in emerald thickets of submerged *Vallisneria* hatched, grew, shed their hard shells, and grew some more. In addition, the stream hosted shimmering schools of striped dace and horny-nosed chubs, all gourmet fare for marauding bands of jut-jawed smallmouth bass, which dominated the habitat with predatory intent.

"See that?" B. J. pointed the tip of his fly rod toward a surface eruption—the silvery flash of terrified minnows leaping to escape a hungry, brown-backed hunter.

Fired with anticipation, we hurried to the shore, where B. J. began to wade in, swishing his line forward and back as he worked a small spinner toward the lair of the feeding fish. I moved on upstream, passing two more pools and riffles to reach a broad, deep, boulder-studded pool, which from the time of the last glacier melt had been inhabited by bass of uncommon size and wariness. Wading in carefully from downstream, I eyed the glassy surface ahead, noting where a bulge and several slow eddies indicated a large boulder hideout. Lengthening the line, I shot a cast over and beyond the bulge, letting my red-and-yellow Mickey Finn streamer fly drift back like a wounded minnow. There was a momentary pause, a twitch on the line, but no solid strike.

"Aha," I thought, "one lies behind yon boulder. I'll rest him a moment and then come back."

Pausing, I craned my neck around and noted the distant plaid-shirted form of B. J. backing toward the shallows, his rod bent in a satisfactory arch against a resisting fish.

With attention directed back to the sunken boulder upstream, I cast the Mickey Finn lightly above the surface bulge, then darted it downstream, stripping line with my left hand. This time, the strike was solid, the hook biting into the lower jaw of the bass, sending fourteen inches of gleaming, red-gilled splendor hurtling skyward. Finding upstream rushes availed little, the fish made an abrupt 180-degree turn, shot past my legs, and headed for the riffle. When he grazed the shallows with his underbelly, he changed his mind and stormed back into the pool. Eventually, the relentless pressure of the bamboo rod wore him down, and he came in reluctantly, doggedly shaking his head. Gripping his lower jaw with thumb and forefinger, I lifted him dripping from the stream, magnificent in his striped tan-and-brown splendor. Since it was a day when no fish were required for supper, the streamer fly was carefully removed, the fish eased back into the river.

During this skirmish, I had become aware of another, much larger fish upriver, which appeared near a heavy thatch of floating vegetation wrapped like green hay around a steel fence post driven into the river bottom. The post supported a single strand of barbed cattle wire about three feet off the water surface. Both ends of the wire stretched to wooden posts on the right and left shores and beyond, where lines of wooden posts containing the conventional three strands of barbed wire were stapled to enclose the farmer's pasture. Had I been a little more observant at the time and a little less intent on the bass, I might have wondered why the three strands on shore became a single strand when stretched across the river, but my pursuit was single-minded. Lengthening the line, I shot a cast toward the eddy curling around the weed thatch, intending to land just to the right of the steel post and under the wire. Unfortunately, my aim was not exact. The Mickey Finn lapped about eighteen inches beyond the wire, then spun backward several times, securely tying itself in place. A few tugs with the rod tip proved futile. Reluctantly, I waded forward, muttering imprecations at the wire, the farmer, milk cows, and the vagaries of fate in general. As I reached to release my streamer fly, I spied the dark form of the bass, perhaps nineteen incredible inches in length, shoot out from under the weed thatch and carve a wake upriver. Thus occupied, I groped for the fly, and brushed the wire with my right hand. The next thing I knew, I landed with a shuddering shock on the seat of my pants in the river, right arm tingling to the shoulder. Stunned, I raised to a sitting position and stared at the wire. It was then that I noticed the white porcelain insulator affixed to the steel post, matched by similar insulators on the wood posts ashore. That darned cattle fence was electrified!

As this was filtering through my stunned brain, I became aware that B. J. had arrived upon the scene. "What possessed you to sit in the river?" he inquired with a derisive snort.

"I got knocked into the river," I answered truthfully.

"Knocked? Who's to knock you down? Hah, you just stumbled backward and went down in a heap," he laughed.

The hilarity did not extend to where I sat shaken, with water swirling around my elbows. "No, listen! I was trying to get my streamer fly off that wire and there is electricity in it."

This brought an even louder guffaw from B. J. "Oh, come now . . ." He shoved his fly rod under his left arm, waded up to the wire, and reached down for the fly. Fascinated, I watched as he made contact, flew backward like he had been struck with a baseball bat, and landed sitting in the river alongside me.

"Ow! Wow!" he screamed. "That wire is charged."

"Exactly . . . I tried to tell you . . . see that white insulator . . ."

"Ow!" B. J.'s hands were shaking, his eyeballs jumping. "Hey, I coulda got killed! If they've got a hundred and ten volts in that wire it would double ground into the water . . . I mighta got hit with two hundred and twenty volts for gosh sakes!"

Slowly we recovered and got to our feet, water dripping from our sodden clothes. "I am going back downstream where it is a darn sight safer," B. J. announced shakily.

"Me, too. There's a heck of a big bass in this pool but he's home free as far as I'm concerned." With that, I gave a hefty jerk on my line, snapped the leader, and left the Mickey Finn dangling from the cattle wire. As far as I know, it may still be there.

Oddly enough, that same stretch of the DuPage River was the scene of another incident one sultry June evening about two years later, almost to the day. George, Don, and I had cut our last afternoon college classes, assembled our tackle, and headed for the river in an aged but dependable Model A Ford belonging to Don's father. Near where we parked was a rusting iron structure spanning the river, known as the Wheatland Bridge, so named because the river at this point bisected Wheatland Township. However, this geographic detail was of no consequence to us. Our interest was focused on a deep pool immediately upriver from the bridge, a pool we knew from experience was populated by a number of medium-to-large smallmouth bass.

First, we were concerned with capturing a sufficient supply of live crawfish in the shallows upstream. In the early summer warmth, the crustaceans were growing rapidly, and in so doing, shedding their hard outer coats. While in the rubbery "soft" stage before the new shells became hardened, they were vulnerable to predation and highly desired by marauding bass. Among river anglers, soft craws are still considered premier baits.

Stalking the shallows in old tennis shoes, pants rolled up above our knees, we each managed to pluck a half dozen soft-shells from the weedy shoals, then hastened back to the big pool to try our luck. For this activity, our fly rods were equipped with six-foot gut leaders—ritually soaked in the river to make them pliable—to which were tied Cincinnati Bass Hooks, size two. The soft crawfish were hooked through the last segments of the tail, then cast with a gentle, swooping, sidearm motion, sending them arching out over the current. The trick, of course, was to make the side cast without having the bait rip off the hook or become looped around the neck of an adjacent angler. In regard to the latter issue, we cautiously spaced ourselves well apart in the water.

Scarcely had our baits landed in the river when Don tensed up. "Got a hit," he hissed, feeding slack with his left hand as the line whistled through the fly rod guides. "Far enough," he muttered. He let the fish pull the line taut, then he hauled back, putting a sharp arch in his bamboo rod. Downriver, a two-pound bronzed form shot skyward, shattering the surface, then crashed back. George and I paused in our efforts, watching as Don battled his bass upstream, foot by foot. It was just as he reached down to retrieve his prize that we heard the rumble of thunder heralding the approach of a storm from the west. A mile away, the tall white spire of the Wheatland Methodist church stood out sharply against a line of purplish black clouds rushing across the green farmland.

At the same time, as though on signal, the bass began feeding with an unusual sense of urgency. While Don hastily impaled his bass on a rope stringer, George and I were engaged with two more. Mine was a ten-inch juvenile, which was quickly subdued, unhooked, and released, and a new bait was impaled. George managed to land his foot-long keeper, and got it strung. By now the rolling line of clouds was no more than a half mile distant. Jagged lightning streaked from cloud to cloud and cloud to ground as the thunder became a near-continuous roar.

Eyeing the approaching storm with apprehension, I reeled in my line and retreated to shore.

"Where you going?" Don asked, feeding slack to another streaking bass.

"I'm going up to the car," I said.

"Are you nuts?" George had laid the hook into his second bass, a head-shaking thirteen-incher that alternated surface acrobatics with underwater feints and rushes. "These fish are really taking off . . . what's a few raindrops?"

Shrugging, I waded up the bank to the pasture and trod through the dusty grass to the fence, slid under the wire, disjointed my rod and climbed into the front seat of the Model A.

A distinct hush had settled over the land as the first wisps of wind-driven black scud raced overhead. From the distance came the tinkle of tiny bells, and the lowing of cattle being herded into barns for evening milking. Birds in fields and trees huddled down, strangely silent. Only the fish appeared to continue their fevered depredations. As I watched George and Don frantically baiting up, handling strikes, and landing fish, my hasty retreat seemed more and more ridiculous. I was reaching for the door handle to get out and return to the river when the world exploded with a blinding flash and a simultaneous deafening crash of thunder. Stunned, my mind took a few seconds to comprehend that lightning had struck the iron bridge. And with that, the heavens let go with a driving torrent of rain.

As I peered through the water-streaked windshield, my first impression of the river was that an incredible number of bass, carp, sunfish, and suckers were writhing on the surface. Next, I made out the forms of my two companions, now on their knees in the stream, frantically attempting to get back on their feet.

Although thoroughly scared, I slid out of the Model A, dove under the wire, and raced to the river bank.

"Omigod!" George bellowed, floundering on knees turned to rubber. Don, eyes wide with terror, jerked upright with his rod in one hand, his other arm windmilling for balance, only to fall backward full length into the river. Dozens of twitching, flopping fish floated past, all stunned by the electrical charge. Apparently, when lightning struck the bridge, it jumped to the river bed and traveled upstream underwater, knocking the entire fish population silly and turning my two friends' legs to noodles.

Throwing caution aside, I splashed into the rain-spattered stream, grabbed George by one arm, and started dragging him toward shore. Don dropped his fly rod and came crawling through the water on his hands and knees. The whole scene suddenly hit me as hilarious, and I began choking with laughter, an activity not shared by my companions.

"What . . . the . . . heck . . . is . . . so . . . doggone . . . funny?" George stuttered through clenched teeth.

Don reached the bank but was still flopping frontward and backward on twitching legs. "Not funny! Not funny! " he yelled, his eyes jumping with shock.

Somehow, I managed to get each one by a shirt sleeve and guided them, stumbling and wobbling, through the rain to the car, the bass on stringers tied to their belts slapping back and forth. Finally, safe inside the Model A and out of the storm, their breathing began returning to normal. Suddenly Don gasped out: "My fly rod! My fly rod is still in the river!"

At that point, nature shattered a firmly believed myth about lightning not hitting the same place twice. A second jagged finger of white light struck the bridge with a deafening boom. Only this time the flash was followed by a glowing ball of white light, which bounded from the bridge abutment to the rain-washed pasture and came skipping toward us like some horrid presence from outer space. Petrified with fright, we watched as the ball bounced past, about a hundred feet away, then collided with a gnarled oak tree, where it exploded like a huge bomb, sending bits of wood and bark flying in all directions.

"Get us outta here!" George screamed, pounding his fist on the dashboard.

Don fumbled with the ignition key, hit the starter, and the Model A lurched down the gravel road through the curtain of rain. By the time we reached the highway, ten miles distant, the clouds were beginning to thin, and patches of blue sky were peering through. Don made a U-turn on the pavement and headed back up the gravel road.

"What the heck are you doing?" George asked.

"Going back to get my fly rod," said Don grimly.

We parked once again by the bridge, got out of the Model A, slid under the barbed wire fence, and walked to the river bank. Don waded out, kicked around in his wading shoes, located his fly rod, picked it up, and came out of the water.

The setting sun glistened on the wet bridge span and turned raindrops into thousands of sparkling glass beads clinging to the pasture grass. The river flowed smoothly, unperturbed, with no sign of the flopping fish that had been so evident during the deluge. Meadowlarks whistled merrily from their fence-post perches; crows cawed from nearby woodlands; the tinkle of tiny bells and the moo of cattle indicated the cows were back in their fields.

All trace of the violent electrical storm had been erased . . . all except the memories burned into our minds and a broad scar on the oak tree where the lightning bolt had exploded.

Thanksgiving Goose

They came off the lake two miles distant with the typical high-pitched honking of Canada geese heading out to feed. My brother-in-law Howie and I had scouted these geese all week, and we thought we had them about figured out.

Each evening the geese came off the refuge just at sunset and flew out to the farm fields, warily circling lower and lower until finally landing to graze for a half hour in corn or soybean stubble. There was an outside possibility of catching them feeding in a field, which might lend itself to a stalk on hands and knees and perhaps a shot. But the best chance for success was to be hidden in the field where they would come to feed again in the morning, just before sunup. If nothing disturbed them the night before, they would invariably land about the same place in the same field. But twice was their limit. The next evening, they would seek out a new feeding area as though aware that hunters' eyes were watching.

On a hazy, drizzly evening, Howie and I were trailing the geese in my old Chevy. Trying to keep the flock in sight, we drove up one graveled road and down the next, while the geese drifted across farm after farm. Eventually, as they circled through the gathering gloom, we lost track of them, forcing us to give up. Wearily I aimed the car for home, resigned, with a too-familiar feeling of defeat.

A half mile ahead appeared the glowing lights of Ray Brechling's gas station, situated on Highway 59. A quick glance at my gas gauge showed the needle crowding empty. I swung off the farm road onto the wet pavement, turned in at the station, and pulled up at a pump.

"Give 'er whatever she'll take," I told Ray as he came out and unscrewed the gas cap.

"Any luck hunting?" Ray nodded toward our gun cases in the back.

"No. We were mostly just looking. We were trailing that big bunch of geese that comes off the lake every night . . . but we lost 'em in the drizzle and darkness."

"I know where they went," Ray grinned. "They doubled back." He waved toward the dark field across the highway. "They may be out there feeding right now."

"No kidding?"

"No kidding. They came in at dark. I could just make them out as they landed on the high ground where the soybean field and the corn stubble come together."

"Anybody shagging them?" Howie asked.

"Nope. In fact, up to a few minutes ago I could hear the clamor out there as they were feeding. He cupped an ear toward the field. Naw. I think they headed back to the refuge."

"Feeding right on top of the high ground?"

"Yep. Dead middle of the field." Ray hung the hose back on the pump and screwed on the gas cap.

"We ought to try for 'em in the morning," Howie suggested. "You want to go with us, Ray? We've got some oversize goose decoys."

"Like to, but I got a transmission job to finish up. If you get a couple of 'em, save me one."

"Yeah." I handed him the cash for the gas. "It's a week to Thanksgiving. What a deal if we could have wild goose with stuffing and cranberries for the holiday." I was sure we would find total approval from my wife, Lil, and my sister, Joyce.

I was totally in error. "What's wrong with turkey?" Lil complained, when we got home. "Turkey is traditional."

"Yeah . . . but wild goose! Wow . . . think about that."

"I'm thinking," she said. "I like turkey better."

"You shoot it, you cook it," said my sister.

Howie shook his head. There were times when women could be unbelievably unreasonable. Still, we went ahead with our plans. Well before dawn the following morning, Howie and I drove to Ray's gas station, now pitch dark and silent. "Ought to leave the car here," I said. "If we park it near the field it might spook the geese."

"Right." Howie was pulling his 12-gauge pump gun out of the back seat.

Before we had headed home the night before, I had counted the fence posts along the road, adjacent to the cornfield. There were fifty-four. With a flashlight, we trudged down the highway, lugging our guns and a dozen plywood Canada goose silhouettes. We counted twenty-seven posts in the flashlight beam. "Oughta be the middle of the field," I noted. "Now we head in." We started for the fence and slid under the wire.

From the road we had more than a quarter mile of walking through frosted, rattling corn stubble to the high point in the field. We hit the rise as the sky in the east was beginning to turn purple. "Going to be a clear, sunshiny day," Howie whispered.

"Yeah," I whispered back.

I don't know why we whispered. The refuge lake where the geese roosted was two miles away.

Hastily we spread out, about fifty yards apart, each of us constructing a small hideaway out of cornstalks where we could lie down and blend in with the stubble. Daylight was coming rapidly as we laid our gloves and guns in the hideaways and clumped up the corn rows to the edge of the soybean stubble. A few goose feathers indicated where the geese might have fed the night before. It was directly upwind from our ambush. Ideal setup.

We quickly arranged the decoys on the frost-coated field. Each decoy was equipped with a long steel pin where the legs would have been. Carefully we pushed the pins through the crusted surface, into the mud, turning each decoy so they would show best from the east, assuming the geese would come in facing a prevailing west breeze. Dawn was coming fast, and as we got the last silhouette stuck in the ground, the faint sound of honking echoed from the distance.

"They're coming off the lake," Howie whispered hoarsely. "Time to get covered up."

Doubled over, we scooted back down the corn rows to our respective hideaways, only mine was missing. I could hear the crackle of cornstalks as Howie hastily covered himself up, but where was my pile of stalks and my gun?

"What the heck are you doing?" Howie hissed.

"I can't find where I hid my gun," I hissed back.

"Oh, for criminey sake!"

In desperation, I sprinted back up the corn stubble and located the first goose decoy I had jammed in the ground. This one, I reasoned, should be directly up the corn row where I laid the gun.

"Honk-ker-honk! Honk-ker-honk!"

The geese were clearly in sight now, coming our way in a wavy line. Dropping to my hands and knees, hoping to be less visible, I frantically scrambled back down the corn row. A glint of blue metal appeared ahead. With a prayer of thankfulness, I slid into my pile of cornstalks and grabbed my double-barreled shotgun. Fortunately, from the air the ground probably appeared dim and dark. At least my scooting about hadn't spooked the geese. They were still boring in on us.

With my back against the frozen ground, I pulled more stalks across my body and a couple over my face. The shotgun rested on my chest, ready if the moment came to shoot.

"KER-HONK! KER-HONK!"

The flock wasn't even going to circle! They were coming straight in, perhaps thirty yards high and dropping. From the breast pocket of my hunting jacket, I pulled out my wood-barreled goose call, put it against my lips, and sent out an answering blast: "KER-HONK! KER-HONK!"

That did it. The front geese cupped their wings and dropped their feet, eyes locked on the dozen phonies standing motionless at the edge of the bean field. Slowly, surely, they let down, but began drifting to my right, away from Howie. It was apparent, if they kept coming, they would be out of range from where Howie was lying, but almost on top of me. I let go of the goose call and stealthily eased my thumb to the shotgun safety. Through the loose covering of cornstalks, I watched intently the approach of the huge water-fowl, the pink of dawn reflected on their grey-and-white bodies, contrasting sharply with their long black necks, black heads, and white throat patches.

"KER-HONK!"

They were so close now I could see the highlights on their black eyes shining in the morning light. "Now!" I murmured half aloud. "It's geese for Thanksgiving dinner!" With one move, I kicked off the cornstalks, rolled over onto one knee and swung the twin bar-rels toward the lead honker. Startled, the geese began frantically flailing air with their wings, crying with alarm.

"Too close," I said to myself. "Wait. Wait and make that first shot a sure one."

There was all the time in the world. With luck, I might even get two. Howie was still prone, but he had raised up on his elbows for a better look. I could well imagine his chagrin at being too far to the right for a shot. Still, he would make a fine witness to my stellar marksmanship as I brought my trophies in for Thanksgiving. The clamoring geese were churning the air with their huge pinions, but now reaching optimum range. Coolly, confidently, I swung on the nearest gander, an enormous bird, picked up his line of flight, swung past the long neck until the head appeared just behind the gold bead front sight, and pulled the front trigger.

Instead of the familiar crash of an exploding shell, there was the continued honking, the whoosh of huge wings. Dumbfounded, I hesitated a split second. "Bum shell . . . didn't fire," my mind registered. "Fire the second barrel."

I swung ahead of the big bird once more and pulled the second trigger. With the same result.

"Shoot, for heaven's sake!" Howie shouted. "Shoot!"

A terrible flash of suspicion shot through my brain. I flipped open the twin barrels and was horrified to see both were empty! In the panic of trying to find my cornstalk hideaway, I had somehow failed to load the gun!

Fumbling frantically in my jacket, I came up with two shells, tried to shove them into the breech and dropped both on the ground. I reached down, grabbed them in exasperation, managed to get them into the twin barrels and snapped the action closed.

It was obvious, however, that the climbing, honking geese were now safely out of range.

Howie was sitting up in the corn to my left, one hand jammed against his jaw in amazement. "What in the world happened to you?"

"Somehow, I forgot to load my shotgun," I confessed.

"You had the only shot. They were out of range for me."

"I know." Sadly, I stood up and stretched my stiff muscles. The geese now formed a typical wedge in the sky and were headed toward the western horizon.

In the glow of the lights at Ray's gas station, we could see a solitary figure in blue-striped overalls standing on the concrete drive-way, legs defiantly apart, hands on his hips. From the distance I heard Ray's booming voice: "WHAT THE HECK WERE YOU DOING? WHY DIDN'T YOU SHOOT?"

I stood silently for a moment, groping for a plausible excuse. Finding none, I simply blurted out the truth: "I FORGOT TO LOAD THE GUN!"

Ray threw both hands in the air, muttered something unintelligible, and stomped into the gas station office.

"I guess we better pick up the decoys," Howie suggested.

"Yeah . . . oh, geez!" Shoulders slumped, I crunched through the frosty stalks to the soybean stubble.

We gathered up the twelve silhouettes and started down the cornfield toward the gas station. The sun was beginning to climb over the eastern horizon in streaks of golden glory. Somewhere in the distance, a rooster crowed. Traffic was moving down the high-way to the hum of tires.

"Well, look at it like this," Howie said at last. "Turkey isn't all that bad."

I nodded, bitterly. Seeking a measure of solace, I recalled the theme of the last Sunday's sermon: "All This, Too, Shall Pass." No matter how tragic, the pastor pointed out, life goes on. But then, I recalled, he was not a hunter.

A Matter of Civic Good

Lil and I drove the Chevy down the grassy lane and into the weedy yard alongside the ramshackle house trailer. We piled out, went around in front, and spied the proprietor hunched on the front steps.

"How ya doin', Charlie?" Lil called out.

The old man turned an uncharacteristically sad stare upon us and spit a stream of brown tobacco juice with unerring aim into one of a half dozen coffee cans placed strategically around the yard. "No darn good," he said.

"What's wrong?"

"All me minnies is dead."

"Your minnows are dead?"

"Yeah . . . they got kilt."

Charlie ran a somewhat irregular live bait business on the river, with minnows his main retail item. If his minnows were dead, he was facing economic disaster.

"What killed 'em?" I inquired.

"P'lution."

"Pollution? Where from?"

"From upriver," Charlie spit another stream of liquid Beech-nut into the closest can and hunched his dried-up frame a little smaller.

For two decades, Lil and I had gotten our live bait from the old river man who eked out a scant existence selling minnows and soft-shelled crawfish during the spring, summer, and fall. He also provided a free and occasionally accurate angler's advisory service. That is, if you purchased some bait and inquired as to where the fish were biting, he would pause thoughtfully, shift his tobacco to the other cheek, gaze upstream and down, and offer his assessment of angling probabilities, like: "Wa-all, if I was goin,' I'd prob'ly head fer them riffles above the Black Road Bridge."

Charlie never asked the world for a whole lot. He had served briefly in the Army during World War I. His tattered discharge certificate was stuck on the wall inside the trailer. And in his younger days, he had been a minor-league pitcher of some note. "Almost went with the White Sox in nineteen twenny-four," he liked to add.

Local legendry held that a fondness for 90-proof rye and a strained arm put him out of baseball. And after an uneven series of jobs, he wound up living in the leaky old riverside trailer, selling live bait. While this provided a rather meager income, it afforded a splendid opportunity for him to pursue his real purpose in life, which was fishing for smallmouth bass. Quite often, anglers would stop by his trailer only to find he had gone fishing; but by mutual agreement they would count out the required number of minnows or crawfish and leave the correct amount of money in a can under Charlie's steps.

And, occasionally, when his bait supply was low, he would draft anyone who showed up as an unpaid assistant to pull the other end of his minnow seine, an activity Lil and I engaged in from time to time. When fortune smiled and we pulled up a net filled with flopping, gleaming chubs, he would let out a happy-go-lucky laugh, which emerged as a long, drawn-out "HAW-W-W!" And then he would spit for emphasis. Somewhere along life's byways he had lost all of his incisor teeth, the frontal gap aiding in controlling the force and direction of the brown stream.

On this particular day, however, he was anything but jovial. "It's that corner upriver by the village bridge . . . the new laundromat an' gas station an' tavern . . . all hooked into that sewer runnin' into the river."

There had been some construction and expansion at an intersection where the highway cut across the river in the small village above, but all of this was supposed to be monitored by health officials.

"Hey, it's against the law to dump stuff in the river," Lil said. "All you've got to do is report it to the state pollution people."

"I done that," Charlie said. "Nothin' happened."

"Did anybody come out to look?"

"I dunno, but the sewage is runnin' outta the pipe and into the river."

"The village has a sewage treatment plant," I pointed out. "Nothing should be going in the river."

"This pipe don't go to the treatment plant. It goes straight to the river."

"You can see it?" I asked.

"Sure . . . you wanna go look?"

I got my hip boots out of the car trunk and shoved my legs in. Lil opted to stay in the car and keep her feet dry.

"We gotta be quiet," Charlie warned as we started out. "I don't want them people to see me pokin' around where their sewer pipe comes out."

The river ran under a bridge through the village, concrete retaining walls sort of sealing the shoreline off from view. Thus we splashed along through the shallows without being observed from above. Charlie stopped by the edge of the last retaining wall, where a brushy slope came to the riverbank. "She's right here," he said, pointing.

The mouth of a twelve-inch glazed tile was visible behind the brush. A grayish-green discharge trickled from the pipe, and a noticeable stench permeated the surrounding atmosphere.

"It wouldn't seem that one pipe could poison the whole river," I said.

"Oh . . . nothin' much comin' out right now." Charlie removed his battered felt hat and mopped his forehead. "But on Saturday afternoon when the laundromat is runnin' full tilt an' on Saturday night when the tavern is jammed full of people, this thing is runnin' like a gusher."

"You say you called the state officials?"

"Yeah, and the county health guys, too."

"Nothing happened?"

"Unh-unh. I think the guy who runs the tavern has got political clout somewhere . . . they never hooked into the village sewage system like they was supposed to."

"Did you see them do that?"

"Sure . . . they just dug a ditch, run the pipe right to the river, an' then covered the whole works up with dirt."

I was thinking about this possible bit of chicanery as we trudged back downriver to the trailer. When I got back in the car, Lil asked, "How did it look?"

"Not too bad, but Charlie says it is a gusher of sewage on Saturdays."

"Can't something be done about it?"

"Well, I've got an idea," I said. After I dropped Lil off at home, I drove several miles east across the farmland to Aukie Lauterbach's big dairy farm. Aukie was in the cow barn getting ready to start milking. "You come out to help me pull teats?" Aukie laughed.

"No, I'll let the machines do that. But I need a bag of oats."

"What for?" Aukie asked.

"Well, old Charlie Fisher down at the bridge has a problem. I need a bag of oats about half the size of a gunny sack."

Aukie thought a minute. "Yeah . . . I think I got a bag the chicken supplement came in." He strode over to the hen house and came back with a cotton sack, took it over to the oat bin, and filled it full.

"You got a piece of baling wire I can wire it shut with?" I asked.

"Sure." Aukie looked mystified. "What's this got to do with Charlie? He ain't got any chickens."

"No. How much do I owe you?"

"Nothing . . . if it's for Charlie. But if you guys are up to something, you don't know where these oats came from."

"I never heard of you, Aukie."

Back at the trailer, I rousted Charlie out. "Do you have a long pole?"

"Sure. I got a clothes pole."

"Get it and let's get going before it gets too dark."

From under the trailer, Charlie retrieved the clothes pole, about twelve feet long. "This O.K.?"

"Perfect. Come on!"

Carrying the oat bag, I led the way silently back upstream, under the bridge, and up to the sewer tile. I slid the bag of oats into the opening, noting with satisfaction that it fit comfortably snug. Then, with the clothes pole, I shoved the oat bag as far up the tile as I could reach. Charlie watched with glittering eyes.

"When those oats soak up, that bag is gonna seal that pipe like concrete," I whispered. Charlie grinned with understanding and spit a brown stream in the direction of the pipe. We returned silently to the trailer, and I drove home.

Work kept me busy for a week, and it was on a Monday that I finally drove back to see Charlie. As I went through the village and past the corner with the laundromat, tavern, and gas station, I noticed a crew of workmen and a couple of backhoes engaged in excavation. When I turned up the lane and stopped at the trailer, Charlie was wearing a bigger grin than usual.

"How's it going?" I asked.

"HAW-W-W!" Charlie laughed and spit. "You shoulda been here last Saturday night!"

"What happened?"

"What happened? Listen. That laundromat was goin' full blast all Saturday evenin', and on Saturday night the tavern was full. You know what people are doin' in a tavern on Saturday night . . . they are drinkin' and goin' to the john and then drinkin' some more . . . " Charlie shook his head in remembrance. "Well, about eleven o'clock, all of a sudden that whole system backed up. The toilets bubbled over like artesian wells, and all hell broke loose. They hadda reg'lar river runnin' down the middle of the tavern and out the screen door . . . men was yellin' and women was screamin' . . . an' then the laundromat let go like Niagara Falls. HAW-W-W!"

He paused, relishing the picture, and then went on: "Well, they hadda shut the whole works down and the next thing, the people in the village was callin' the state and county health people, and they come out and had 'em dig it all up . . . right down to where the pipe bypassed the village sewer system. I guess they figgered to save a little money, but now they got to do it all over again, and it's gonna cost 'em a lot more."

I grinned and gave Charlie a poke on the shoulder. "We don't know anything about it, do we?"

He spit an extra-long stream of Beechnut and looked me straight in the eye. "HAW-W-W! You know what we are, Bob?"

"No . . . what are we?"

"We're just a couple of envir'nmental do-gooders . . . that's what. HAW-W-W!"

The Irish Rebellion

Rusty was the orneriest piece of dog flesh that ever got concealed inside a sleek cover of mahogany Irish setter fur. It was difficult to understand how such an absolutely handsome field dog could be so utterly full of hate. Hate for everybody and everything. Just flat mean. Of course, some hunters said his owner, my old hunting buddy George, was equally ornery, but that was an inaccurate impression. George was simply single-minded when it came to bird hunting. He focused entirely on the matter at hand and brooked no outside distraction. If, for instance, he was hunting bobwhite, he concentrated his energies on that endeavor with fierce intensity. When Rusty was on point, no one in his right senses would get anywhere near the dog, or he might get bit. Nor should one stray between the dog and George, or he was apt to have a charge of size-eight chilled shot go whoosh past his head when the birds flushed. No, one hunted carefully with George, one eye on him and one eye on the ranging setter. And one did not reach down in a lax moment to stroke the noble head of the dog . . . not unless one wished to draw back a thoroughly lacerated hand.

Along with some bitter criticism of the dog, among friends in our immediate gunning circle, a few asserted that George would occasionally indulge in deception, perhaps bordering on treachery.

If, for instance, they declared, Rusty was on point, perhaps on the far side of a fencerow where only George could see him, George would not necessarily call attention to this fact until he flushed the birds and got the first shot on the rise. However, any experienced hunter will recognize that as a fair maneuver: he who owns the dog is entitled to the first shot if the other hunter is not attentive.

Oddly enough, except for his regal bearing, Rusty was totally unlike his father, a sturdy Irishman named Jack. Jack was a methodical, friendly, even-tempered hunter and a classic retriever. Jack's only drawback was a well-developed disdain for poor marksmanship. If a hunter missed an easy shot, Jack would stare at the offender with unmistakable reproach. Two missed shots, Jack would lose all enthusiasm for the hunt and would likely leave the field, trot back to the car, lie down, and take a nap. No amount of threats or cajoling would get him to stir any more that day.

Rusty, on the other hand, was eager, high-strung, hyper. He would hunt from dawn to dark without a letup, as though almost in a fury. He not only hated strangers, he barely tolerated George's few close friends. Some of our shooting acquaintances blamed George for this disorder; but more likely, it was the result of a traumatic childhood. Rusty grew up in a backyard kennel adjacent to a busy residential thoroughfare. There was a grade school just down the block, and some of the less principled little moppets were wont to taunt him, rattle sticks against his fence, and engage in any other deviltry aimed at driving the dog wild. By the time George and his family moved out to dwell on a small farm, Rusty had become manic, treacherous, ready to take the leg off the postman, newspaper delivery boy, or anyone else he could reach.

On the hunt, Rusty would tolerate other gunners as long as they kept their distance. On point, he would bare his teeth if a guest hunter came too near and would retrieve only to George, no matter who shot the bird. But even then, he retrieved only with a grudging reluctance and exhibited an air of possessiveness as though all birds he pointed were, by legal right, his to keep; he was as surly and hard-mouthed as a snapping turtle. Given George's mental makeup, hunting with those two was like being next to a war waiting to break out.

It was a crisp October day when I drove through groves of russet oaks and yellow-orange maples into the lane leading to George's farm on the sand bluffs overlooking the Mississippi River. It is an area a little farther north than bobwhite normally range, an unusual combination of cover and climate where an unusual number of coveys dwell in brier, buckwheat, and sorghum patches interspersed among scrub oak, maple, and cedar. George discovered this upland gunner's bonanza after spending countless hours pursuing those stubby, feathered rockets . . . one reason he bought the farm where he lived.

When I turned into the yard, George was splitting wood by the garage. He paused, ax in hand, nodding recognition. Rusty, as usual, set up an ear-splitting din from behind his wire enclosure. George shouted a few choice threats to subdue the dog, jammed the ax in the splitting block, and strode over, hand outstretched.

"Been a long time," he said.

"Got a wife and two little kids now," I replied. "Can't go gallivanting around the country like I used to. How's the bird population?"

"Located eight, maybe ten, coveys along the bluffs." He looked toward the river. "There's some brier in there, so wear tough pants."

"How's Rusty?"

George stiffened, eyes narrowed. "If he didn't have the best nose in the county, I'd kill that black-hearted spawn of Satan." Then he shrugged and waved toward the house. "Better get your clothes changed."

Having hunted uplands with George off and on for several decades, I was aware of his preference for terrain that would discourage all but the most hardy and dedicated of gunners. In the house, I changed to heavy canvas pants, leather boots, and a canvas coat with pockets comfortably weighted with shells. Within a half hour, we were striding up the first ridge, Rusty ranging ahead, reddish coat gleaming in the autumn sun. From the distance, he was the classic picture of a hunting setter, but up close he appeared even more surly than the last time we hunted, and I gave him ample berth.

"Point!" George called softly. Rusty was anchored, nose forward, by a clump of brier. Whrrr . . . Whrrr . . . six bobs went airborne and we managed a bird apiece. Thereupon followed a ritual we have followed for lo, these many years: we paused in the bright sun, shotgun barrels crooked over our arms, comparing our stubby trophies. A bobwhite in hand is a cause for respect, bordering on awe: not only for their speed and deceptive flight, but for their delicately patterned, colorful plumage. Indeed, I felt we were lucky to have two birds to compare. At least two—relatively intact. The first half-hearted retrieve had elicited a plethora of colorful curses from George. The second involved a snarling tug-of-war between man and dog. Rusty growled and glared with venom before he finally released the last bobwhite. Let it be recorded that George did a little glaring and growling of his own.

At the edge of a buckwheat patch, Rusty came on point again, locked in place like a reddish brown statue. The sight was magnificent . . . as long as one did not forget the unsocial personality of the creature involved. George moved in easily on the left, and I eased closer on the right, guns at ready. The birds held until the last second, exploding almost from under our feet in a thunder of blurred pinions. George, always a dead shot, dropped one on the rise and doubled as the covey leveled off across the grain field. I missed an easy first shot but covered my embarrassment by dumping one in a puff of feathers with the second barrel. At the command "Fetch!"

Rusty bolted to the first bird, picked it up, and then paused as though to consider.

"Fetch, dang you, you misbegotten son of a hyena!" George shouted. Rusty sauntered over with studied insolence, eventually spitting out the bird. The second bobwhite took a lot more time. Instead of coming directly back, the dog circled around as though debating whether to deliver it or swallow it.

"Fetch, you red bag of pig dung!" George screamed. Rusty stood ten yards away, eyes gleaming with pure hatred. Eventually he moved close enough for George to grab his collar and then pinch his muzzle. With one move, the dog coughed up the bird and ripped a streamer of canvas from George's coat sleeve. Then, in a torrent of invective from George, he headed back for the last bird, growling every step.

"That did it!" George snarled, inspecting his torn sleeve. "That's the final straw!"

I stood transfixed, awaiting the next explosion of violence.

Rusty picked up the last bird and started to walk away with it. "FETCH!"

The dog shook, but stopped.

"FETCH . . . DANG . . . YOU!"

Rusty turned and took two steps in our direction, eyes blazing. George moved slowly toward the dog, hand outstretched. The growl in Rusty's throat got louder and meaner. A string of saliva dripped from his chin. I began getting extremely edgy, like a United Nations peacekeeper implacably caught between bitter enemies. At length, George maneuvered within reach of the setter, dropped his shotgun, and dove forward, grabbing the dog's head. What happened next was almost too fast for the eye to follow. Rusty spit out the bird and then sprang full force at George's face. In a sharp reflex, George threw up his forearm, but the force of Rusty's charge knocked him backward to his knees. Canine teeth flashing, the dog dove for the kill, but was stopped by another forearm blow. The dog clamped down on the arm, and the two went around and around in a fury of flying dust, snarls, and tearing fabric. Overcoming my astonishment, and fearing for George's life, I threw up my shotgun, but couldn't risk a shot at the dog in that flying debris without hitting them both.

The battle surged back and forth in a wide circle, George desperately struggling to get back on his feet, yelling threats of murder and mayhem, the dog ripping and tearing at him and keeping him off balance. With blood streaming down his knuckle, George suddenly connected with a haymaker that staggered the dog for an instant. Still on his knees, George followed up with a tremendous kick, his right boot smacking Rusty solidly alongside the head, sending the dog end-for-end into the buckwheat.

The setter rolled over twice and lay gasping, sweat-streaked flanks convulsing. George staggered upright, wiped his lacerated hand on his tattered jacket. Eyes burning, he picked up his shotgun and fingered the trigger. Rusty snarled but didn't move. I was transfixed, fearful that I would be witnessing an execution. Instead, George shakily picked up the bedraggled bobwhite from the dust, hurled it into the cover, and shouted: "FETCH!"

With a low growl, the dog pulled himself painfully erect, limped toward the bird, picked it up, and retrieved it flawlessly to George's hand. For a moment the dog and hunter glared at each other; then George stuffed the stubby bundle of feathers into his hunting coat, picked up his cap from the ground, snapped it forcefully onto his head, and wiped his shotgun with a tattered sleeve. Chest heaving, he gasped at the dog, "All right, you red-haired bucket of venom . . . now, let's hunt!"

With another low growl, Rusty limped across the buckwheat, George stalking resolutely behind. I caught up with George and eyed his torn coat and bleeding hand. "That dog really got you," I observed.

"Yeah," George spit out, breath whistling in his throat. "One of these days . . . it's gonna be him or me." He squinted at the setter ranging back and forth in front of us. "I'd kill him . . . but he's still got the best nose in the whole dang county."

Brown Trout and Other Problems

Like many of our ancestors who came to these shores from other lands, the brown trout, *Salmo trutta*, arrived in America from Europe in the 1800s. But unlike our immigrant predecessors who often came as described by poetess Emma Lazarus on the Statue of Liberty: " . . . your tired, your poor . . . the wretched refuse of your teeming shore . . . ," the brown trout was and is an aristocrat, the royalty of Old World fisheries. And for many North American anglers the species continues to hold a position of princely esteem. In addition, this majestic warrior is extremely tough and highly adaptable to a variety of habitats. It thrives in hundreds of streams not acceptable to our native brookies. Furthermore, most anglers who seek him out credit the brown with the ultimate in sagacity, a trait that ensures the species' survival in heavily fished waters. The wariness of the brown is admittedly matched only by the deviousness of those who seek him. Brown trout anglers are notoriously lacking in truth and will resort to any falsehood or subterfuge in order to avoid giving accurate information on streams where the species thrives. Fortunately, a number of years ago I was enabled, through clever dialogue, to extract the location of several good brown trout waters from extremely creditable but devious sources whose normal guile was somewhat impaired through the liberal application of certain beverages. The list of streams included the Little Roche A Cri near Neceedah, Wisconsin.

Not long after obtaining this information, my family pulled our camping trailer into a pleasant park in Adams County, beachhead for an assault on the local waters. As was our custom, we first reconnoitered the campground, locating such critical facilities as drinking water and toilets, a search that also revealed a thriving stand of poison ivy. In my Boy Scout days, the Beaver Patrol once camped overnight in a thicket of the noxious weed, and all came down with rash and blisters except myself. Over time, other incidents of exposure made me aware that I was one of those extremely rare persons with an immunity to the poison. This fortunate circumstance provided a means of earning spending money during my youth through uprooting the plants by hand from around my aunt's and her neighbors' summer cottages on the Fox River.

Thus it was that I fearlessly plucked a modest bouquet of poison ivy plants and took them back to our camping trailer to show my wife and two daughters, explaining how to identify the weed by its three-leaf clusters, describing in graphic detail the distressing symptoms of the disease. Further, I issued a fatherly warning that it was unlikely they had inherited such rare immunity as I possessed and that they should therefore avoid contact with the weed at all costs. They were, of course, properly impressed by my studied nonchalance while handling the plants.

That done, I began assembling my tackle, determined to seek the entree for a trout dinner. Lil and the kids elected to remain at the campsite, where a sand beach beckoned. With a shrug, I shoved my equipment into the family car and, accompanied by a detailed county map, sought out the nearby trout haunts.

The Little Roche A Cri, carving its course through sand and

clay, turned out to be a rather disappointing, turbid stream, heavily overhung with willows and other hardwoods. June rains had added to the murkiness of the water and also to the slippery footing along the shore. My first impression was that my informants had carefully led me astray. However, as all trout prospectors know, appearances can be deceiving. With critical eye, I stalked carefully along, scrutinizing the stream surface for any sign of piscatorial activity. It was when thus studiously engaged that I was suddenly struck a tremendous, paralyzing blow to my right rib cage, driving me to my knees. My initial thought was of an ambush engineered by hostile natives armed with bows and arrows. A hasty investigation revealed that no fletched shaft protruded from my side, but that my wound had been inflicted by the handle of my landing net carried on an elastic thong from the rear of my fishing jacket. Somehow, as I followed the streamside trail, the net mesh had become snagged on a branch, the elastic cord had stretched to the maximum, and then the mesh had slipped loose, allowing the handle of the net to fly back with incredible force. Attempting to recover my breath while sitting on a trailside log and ruefully rubbing my wounded ribs, I found my attention captured by a swirl on the water upstream. In a spot where the current narrowed between two fallen willow trees, a trout of substantial proportions came up, slurped a floating insect, and vanished. Concern over my wound quickly vanished. With stealth, I approached within casting distance and spied a second rise, no doubt the same fish, and certainly worth of attention.

The problem was, there was no apparent way to reach the fish. The two fallen willows upstream prevented floating a fly down to the rising fish. Secondly, a similar cluster of overhanging branches blocked access from downstream. Where I was standing, there was a nearly vertical six-foot drop down an eroded clay bank to the water. While pondering these hazards, I saw the trout come up again, exhibiting a certain reckless contempt. It was readily apparent that any effort to slide down the bank to the stream might well result in a fast skid to oblivion. The roily waters gave no indication of how deep the stream might be, if it had any bottom at all. However, from my location on the lip of the slope, it appeared that an upstream side cast might be made by working the line back and forth at waist level, and the fly laid out to drop, with some luck, into the current between the half-submerged willows.

It is well known that large browns are inveterate cannibals; thus I selected a size six streamer, created by the Weber tackle people at Stevens Point, Wisconsin, to imitate a baby brown trout. This I tied to the thread-thin leader tippet, and I began working out line, sidearm, horizontal to the water surface. After a dozen failures, I was fortunate enough to lay out a satisfactory cast, the fly landing about four feet above the rise zone. Without hesitation, the brown rolled up in a golden flash, sucked in the streamer, and dove.

Although I hadn't expected a strike on the first float, my reflexes drove the hook home, and the rod whipped into an arc while I concentrated on keeping the surging fish from diving into the upstream willow coppice. At length, my head-shaking adversary tired, reversed direction, and headed down the current, where it took every ounce of my skill to keep it out of the downstream willow thicket. Eventually, the relentless pressure of the rod brought the struggling trout back to a point six feet directly below my feet, where it lay wallowing against the steep, wet, clay bank. The situation appeared almost impossible. From my location atop the steep bank, there was no way to reach the fish with the net. Nor was my leader strong enough to hoist it up.

As I eyed the trout, one gleaming side half out of the water, the germ of a plan evolved in my mind. Perhaps, I reasoned, it might be possible to ease my way down this steep bank headfirst, inching along, digging my fingers into the clay, until I could reach my prize and somehow flip it up on the bank behind me. Then, with dexterity and luck, I might be able to scuttle my way up backward, like a crawfish, to level ground. The risk of losing my purchase and skidding headlong into the stream was readily apparent, but the old adage "nothing ventured, nothing gained" assumed overriding proportions. Dropping my rod on the grass and gripping the taut leader in my teeth, I began my headfirst descent. Every foot or so, I paused with the fingers of my left hand anchored in the clay, and with my right hand I drew the leader through my teeth, keeping it tight against the fish. Eventually, I worked my way down to where I was stretched out full length, upside down on the clay slope, the trout and I virtually eye to eye. Once again I made sure the fingers of my left hand were jammed into the clay to the knuckles, then I reached down with my right hand, gripped the slippery trout firmly behind the gills, spit the leader out of my mouth, and hurled the fish over my shoulder and upward with all the force I could muster. A satisfactory solid thump on the sod above indicated my throw had been accurate. However, this sense of accomplishment was immediately overshadowed by the realization that I would now have to somehow work my way up the slippery bank feet-first, a ticklish confrontation with the forces of gravity.

With a squadron of hungry mosquitoes now attacking my unprotected, sweat-streaked face, I began the critical backward ascent. Short of breath and with my injured ribs emitting flashes of pain, I somehow managed to inch backward up the clay slope, slide over the grassy rim, and collapse on the sod. After a few moments, I struggled upright and inspected my catch, a truly magnificent specimen of nineteen inches, its burnished golden flanks dotted with red and black spots. Under most circumstances, I would have slipped the hook free and released the fish, but not this time, not after such an ordeal. "Listen you," I addressed the fish. "You have put me through considerable trial, old trout, but, God willing, you will provide my little family with a brown trout supper tonight."

Some time later, with the fish baking over coals in a foil pouch, garnished with bacon strips and slices of onion, I related in detail to my wife and kids how I outwitted this wily denizen of the Little Roche A Cri, retrieved it upside down, and endured considerable pain in the process.

"Weren't you afraid of falling into the stream?" Lil inquired.

"Yes," I replied," but I was more afraid another angler might come along and observe me creeping headfirst down that clay bank, conclude that I had somehow lost my sanity, and summon the authorities."

"He could have made a good case," Lil agreed.

Accompanied by mashed potatoes, fresh peas from a store in town, and an apple compote for dessert, the trout dinner approached gourmet dimensions. We consumed every morsel. And that would be the end of the story, except that the trip had an aftermath.

Some six days later, when we arrived home, I broke out with a case of hives. I have had hives before, and normally I would have simply waited for the symptoms to abate. But these persisted and seemed to be growing more acute. At the urging of my wife, I made an appointment and visited our local medical practitioner, Frank Bender, M.D.

"Doc," I said, "what do you prescribe for hives?"

"Hives?" Doc gave me a skeptical look and checked the itching rash, which now extended up the inside of my arms and down my legs. "Um," he said. "Um . . . hunh. Been out camping lately?"

"Yeah . . . up in Wisconsin . . . let me tell you about a nifty brown trout about twenty-one inches long I took on a streamer fly up on the . . . ah . . . "

Doc waved off my story and put away his stethoscope. "Contact dermatitis," he announced.

"What?"

"Contact dermatitis . . . poison ivy."

"Poison ivy? Of course I saw lots of poison ivy. I even showed some to my family so they wouldn't get into it. However, I am immune to poison ivy. I even pulled it up around the cottages when I was a kid."

"Um-hunh," Doc said. "I'm going to tell you something. There is no such thing as an immunity to poison ivy. Some people get it easier than others, but anyone can get poison ivy if the circumstances are right." He paused while I put my shirt back on. "I'm going to give you a prescription for medication you can put on the rash and the blisters. Don't wash the affected spots with bath soap and water, it will just spread it around. Take it easy for a few days and keep the medication on it . . . should clear right up."

The itching discomfort was the least of my problems. After a brief stop at Krebs Drug Store for the required ointment, I had to return home and face my family.

"What did the doctor say?" Lil inquired as I came though the door.

"He prescribed some medication."

"No . . . I mean, what did he say you've got?"

"If you must know, I've got a case of poison ivy."

There was a brief moment of silence. Then the house exploded with hoots of mirth. Even to this day, whenever the subject of poison ivy comes up in a conversation with friends or neighbors, one of the kids is certain to announce, "Oh, Daddy is immune!" And then collapse in laughter.

I think the behavior experts are right. Kids today don't have the consideration for their elders that they did when I was young.

The Wendigo

On a segment of the Minnesota-Ontario border, fourteen-mile-long Crooked Lake pours over Curtain Falls in a thunder of foam into a series of churning rapids leading to Iron Lake. The falls and surrounding granite-rimmed gorge are preferred subjects for photography by modern-day canoe paddlers, who portage around the cascade on a trail worn smooth over centuries by thousands of bare feet, moccasins, and boots. This portion of the ancient voyageurs' fur route offers a scene of incredible beauty. It is also a scene of danger. The Ojibwa people believe it is the home of a wendigo, the most feared evil spirit in their culture. Indisputably, it has been a scene of disaster for the unbelieving or the unwary.

In September 1963, Lil and I were at Curtain Falls completing a movie about canoe country camping. We had ample footage of paddling, fishing, fire building, and cooking. What we seemed to need was some type of spectacular shot to cap off the film, something much more dramatic than a lone canoeist paddling off into the sunset. We were standing on the portage viewing the falls when a sudden inspiration took hold. "Suppose," I said to Lil, "that you take the camera and set up on the rocks below the first rapids and I take the canoe, circle below the falls, and then shoot the rapids."

Rain had fallen for two solid weeks, and the falls presented an awesome view, the rapids a maelstrom of churning froth. Lil looked over the scene, frowning with considerable doubt. "It looks really rough," she cautioned. "If the canoe gets busted up, it's forty-five miles back to our car at Crane Lake."

"Ah . . . it's not as bad as it looks . . . lots of suds . . . lots of noise. But I've got a route figured through." The adrenaline was pumping. At age forty-two, experienced and trail-hard, I had no room in my lexicon for fear or doubt. "Let's do it."

Lil reluctantly lugged the 16mm Bolex and tripod to a rocky point just downstream from the rapids and got set up. I took one last look to make sure everything was in place and was just about to push the canoe off when a familiar voice at my elbow said: "What are you doing, Bob?"

I turned to meet the stolid mahogany visage of Native American wilderness guide Stanley Owl, who was portaging canoes and gear for a group of fishermen.

"We're shooting a movie," I said.

"I see that." Stan's dark eyes flickered over the scene. "But what are YOU doing?"

"Uh . . . well . . . " I realized Stanley would not approve my venture. "I'm going to take the canoe by myself up around the base of the falls so I'll be kind of silhouetted against the foam . . . then take the main current and shoot the rapids past the camera."

"Can't do that," Stanley stated evenly.

"What do you mean 'I can't?' "

"There's a wendigo in those rapids," Stanley replied without a flicker of emotion.

"Wendigo? Ah, come on, Stan, that's a lot of old Indian superstition . . . you don't believe in that stuff, do you?"

Stan's eyes flickered a trifle. "Five years ago, a Forest Service ranger and I tried to run it. The canoe got torn apart and we both got smashed up pretty bad. He was in the hospital for three weeks."

"That wasn't any wendigo, you guys just screwed up."

"No . . . " Stan said softly. "There's something in there. You can't make it, Bob." He eyed the life jacket I had lying loose on the bottom of the canoe. "You better put that on," he added.

"It would look bad in the movie, Stan . . . besides, I'm used to whitewater . . . I don't need it." At this point in my life I was not in the habit of backing away from a challenge, natural or otherwise, and was certainly well supplied with confidence. Perhaps a trifle oversupplied. My concluding statement to my somber friend was "Well, you just watch me, Stan!" With a laugh, I pushed off, well aware that in addition to Lil and Stanley, I had a quartet of anglers on the portage above to witness my performance.

It all started out gloriously. Kneeling just behind the center thwart, I boldly guided my fifteen-foot Grumman around the base of the falls, where the sun glittered on the spectacular, thundering cascade. More than before, I was certain that this would provide a magnificent final scene to our film. Then I swung with powerful strokes into the mainstream and headed with assurance for the "V" where the current accelerated and plunged between two glacier-scarred ledges into a cauldron of churning suds.

I still cling tenuously to the thought that I might have made it if it hadn't been for that final gust of wind that grabbed the bow and swung the canoe slightly off course. Upon reflection, however, I can't be sure it was the wind that grabbed the bow. Certainly, something did. In any event, instead of hitting the "V" dead center, the canoe ricocheted off the top of the right-hand ledge, then plunged nose-first straight down into the froth. Instinctively, I dropped the paddle, grabbed both gunwales, and shoved my head beneath the protection of the center thwart as both the canoe and I were swallowed up in froth.

There was a tremendous jolt as the canoe smashed into the rocky bottom bow-first, momentarily knocking me loose from my grip; but I managed a desperate grab, catching the left gunwale with both hands, although my body was now at the mercy of the current outside the hull. The impact had torn a gaping hole in the bow flotation section and shattered two ribs, but I had no knowledge of that as the canoe and I went whanging and crunching over the underwater rocks.

An old rule says that if a canoe swamps, the best course of action is to stay with the craft. And under most circumstances, this is a useful precept to follow, but not when half of the canoe has ceased to float. I was desperately clinging to the broken bow section and had no idea what was wrong as my half of the wounded craft failed to rise back to the surface. In all this I was acutely aware of a terrible, violent presence that ripped my wool shirt from the left pocket to the belt, slashed my left pant leg, and viciously slammed my shins and knees. At the same time it sounded like teeth grinding up the aluminum.

Panic-stricken, I struggled for a breath of air; I reversed my grip on the gunwales and pulled myself hand-over-hand to the stern, which was still partially afloat. I managed one desperate gasp of air, and then the canoe and I went over the crest and plunged into the next churning rapids.

It is amazing how fear can motivate the human species. Once my head broke surface the second time, I hastily abandoned ship, struck out for shore, and managed to clamber shakily up the bank, aware of blood leaking from both knees and my left shin.

Stan already had his canoe loose and was paddling across to retrieve me. He didn't say a word as I scrambled aboard, just tossed me a paddle. We maneuvered alongside my damaged craft and towed it to the shore, where we managed to muscle it stern-first up to the portage while water poured out of the ripped bow. We found a flat spot and began to assess the damage as a white-faced Lil appeared with the first aid kit to patch up my cuts.

Stan located a couple of smooth, round rocks and handed one to me, indicating with his hands that we would hammer the bent aluminum back into some semblance of order. With me holding my rock against the hull on the inside and with Stan pounding on the outside, we went at it like body-and-fender specialists. In a few minutes, we got the worst dents and rips pounded back into hull shape. Lil dug a dry towel and two rolls of duct tape from the duffle, and after drying the outside, we taped the tears in the aluminum. This done, I thanked Stanley for his help. He shrugged, said nothing, and went back to finish getting the fishermen across the portage.

We couldn't do anything about the broken ribs, which left the leaky bow segment of the canoe loose as a soggy noodle, but Lil and I did manage to get the canoe back to Crane Lake and our car. Even though Lil's grandmother was Ojibwa and certainly knew about wendigos, Lil was kind enough not to say a whole lot when Stan was present; but on the way to Crane Lake, she told me she had been terrified when the canoe and I vanished into the foam and was sure an evil spirit had killed me when only a short section of the stern reappeared. She didn't see me get out of the current and only realized I had survived when she saw me in Stan's canoe. And she made it plain that she didn't think my escapade was particularly brilliant, especially after Stan's warning, and added that I had better not defy the spirits again. Under the circumstances, there was nothing much to debate. I kept my mouth shut.

We didn't see Stanley again until just before Thanksgiving. We were coming down the front steps of the post office, and Stan was approaching from across the street. I waved a greeting as he drew near, but he showed no recognition until he stepped up on the sidewalk. Expressionless as usual, he glanced at me and said softly: "Run any more rapids, Bob?"

Lil and I simply doubled up laughing. When I finally got my

breath back, I replied: "No, Stan . . . I'm staying out of the rapids."

And in a more serious vein, I added, "You are right about that piece of water. There IS a wendigo living in those rapids and he had me good . . . but I got lucky . . . very, very lucky . . . and got away."

Stan stared straight into my eyes for a moment, nodded, managed just a wisp of a smile, and walked up the steps into the post office.

Pop Dixon

"D'ye hae any fr-rogs, laddie?"

The bushy-browed, crusty old Brit with a broad Northumberland accent sat in the boat, eyeing our lightweight spinning tackle with a mixture of suspicion and disdain.

"No . . . no frogs," I replied, "but we've got something just as good or better."

At that comment, the bushy eyebrows shot up, and the eyes beneath changed from suspicion to pure disbelief: "Wha' manner-r o' bait would ye be refer-rin' to?"

"Jigs and plastic grubs."

"Ah, noo, laddie." The old man shook his head. "If ye intend to get yoursel' some fish in this lake, ye'll need live fr-rogs."

He had been introduced to us as "Pop" Dixon, an import to Canada from that part of northern England near the Scottish border. At the conclusion of World War II, he had migrated across the Atlantic, eventually settling on the shore of Manitoba's Falcon Lake, eighty-two miles east of Winnipeg. A pine-rimmed gem of Canadian Shield water, Falcon Lake is a favored playground for Winnipeg's outdoor-minded set. Provincial tourism official George Marsh had steered Lil and me there because of its fine sand beaches, excellent accommodations, and a third, well-hidden asset: a thriving population of thick-bodied smallmouth bass.

Indeed, George drove with us over to Falcon Beach Motel, where we obtained accommodations, had lunch, and assembled our spinning tackle. "I've got a guide to take you out this afternoon," George confided. "He's a brusque old character with a heavy accent, kind of set in his ways; but he knows more about the fish in this lake than anyone else around."

Unfortunately, George had given no indication that Pop was a frog specialist. Had this been the case, we might have visited a neighborhood bait shop and secured a supply. However, we were now standing on the motel dock, ready to go, and the afternoon was on the wane. It was no time for debate.

With Pop in the outboard runabout tied to the dock was the owner of the boat, a lakeside summer resident named Eddie, who said little but looked on the frog discussion with bright-eyed interest . . . like someone who had obtained the last ticket to a popular Broadway show. Lil and I felt a trifle awkward, standing in the sun, tackle in hand, as Pop glowered and lectured on frogs while Eddie grinned and watched. We had not yet been invited to step aboard.

"Where would you fish if we had some frogs?" I finally ventured.

"Whoosh!" exclaimed the old man, waving a gnarled hand in the direction of the entire lake. "The bays, the points, the r-reefs out yonder-r . . . but I'll tell ye 'tis noo use to tr-ry. These fish'll noo bite except on fr-rogs."

Eddie at last motioned Lil and me to climb in, which we quickly did and settled back against the cushioned seats. Pop stoked his black briar pipe with exasperation, put a match to the bowl, drew a deep breath, and fired out an immense cloud of blue smoke. As the boat revved up and then carved a wake through the water, it was obvious Pop was resigned to a wholly worthless afternoon. At length he poked Eddie and gestured listlessly toward a small, tree-lined bay. Eddie nodded, throttled down, and let the watercraft coast to within casting range.

The lines of disapproval deepened on Pop's face as he watched us tie on yellow-bodied jigs. It should be noted here that the time frame was the late 1950s. Jig-and-plastic-bodied lures had taken the bass-filled southern impoundments by storm, but were barely starting north. Two months previously, Lil and I had scored on large-mouth bass on Arkansas' Bull Shoals Lake; we surmised that the same jig lures would also devastate northern smallmouth, especially since they had never seen these baits and had no reason to be wary.

"And what might ye call thot?" Pop pointed at the yellow lure now attached to my monofilament.

"Jig and grub," I replied, swinging the bait in his direction.

"Whoosh!" Pop inspected the lure at arm's length as though not wishing to become contaminated. "Noo cr-r-eature in his r-r-ight mind would dar-re touch it," he affirmed.

In the meantime, Lil had fired a cast at a half-submerged cedar tree that angled down into the lake from the shoreline. Her lure sank momentarily, then she picked up the slack and jigged it up-ward. The line snapped taut, the rod arched, and the drag let out a groan of protest. Three pounds of enraged smallmouth bass broke the surface, hung suspended for a split second, then crashed back-ward. Pop's head jerked around in astonishment.

"Aye, there, lassie. Might ye be tied into somethin'?"

Lil nodded, gaining a little line on the churning fish. Eddie shoved an aluminum-handled landing net toward Pop, who got onto his feet with some difficulty. "It's me left hip," he confided. "Courtesy of his honor-r, Gener-r-al R-r-ommel." With that, he limped to the side of the boat, poised the net over the surface, and then wrapped the bass in the mesh with a single swoop. He lifted the dripping prize from the net and handed it to me.

"Nice bass," I commented, holding the gleaming fish for Lil to admire. I removed the hook from its jaw and slid it quickly back into the lake.

"'Ere, now!" Pop growled. "Have ye lost your-r senses, laddie?"

"What's wrong?"

"W'ot's wrong? Ye put yer bass back in the lake. If ye should be for-r-tunate enough to get anoother-r bass on yer rubber-r doo-dad, put it on the stringer, eh? We're supposed to have fish for-r supper-r."

Shortly thereafter, a second bass took my jig and was subsequently boated after a satisfactory fight. Pop produced a rope stringer, impaled the fish through both lips, and swung it over the side. When he had the stringer secured to a boat cleat, he leaned nearer. "D'ye mind if I hae a look at your-r bait, laddie?"

This time he inspected the lure very closely, testing the hook point with his thumb, pinching the plastic body. "Could ye figur-re any fish in his r-right mind gr-rabbin' somethin' so ootlandish?"

As luck would have it, it was one of those days when the bass, as Pop noted, "went daft." It seemed like every bay, every rock pile, and every point was teeming with brown bodies, all hell-bent on committing hari-kari. If Lil didn't have a fish on, I did. Sometimes both of us together. The stringer built up to ten fine brown-backed specimens, ranging from fifteen to nineteen inches. Then we released the rest without a protest from Pop. However, one more time he grabbed my lure, stared at it quizzically and muttered, "Incr-r-edible."

At five P.M. Eddie noted we had best head back to the dock. "Got to get these bass ready for supper," he pointed out.

It is not easy to quit when the action is furious, but we were highly satisfied with the day's results and certain that Falcon Lake had a well-deserved, yet not widely advertised, reputation for quality angling.

When we hit the dock, Pop limped out of the boat and lifted the stringer of bass for all to see. "Whoosh!" he called to the motel guests—some in the water, some lazing on the beach or stretched out in beach chairs. "Come see what these Yanks have managed . . . and with the wor-r-ld's most incr-r-edible bait!"

Within moments, he had collected a large audience, which inspected our catch with frequent oohs and aahs as Pop turned the stringer first this way, then that, in the late afternoon sun. All the while he kept exclaiming, in colorful detail, about how we did it with the "incr-redible" bait.

"Ever-ry one was caught on this wee plastic beastie!" he affirmed, holding one of our yellow jigs aloft with his free hand.

But suppertime was near, and Eddie broke up the gathering. "Come on, Pop," he urged. "Let's get the fish filleted, eh?"

The old man nodded, and they headed for the screened fish house. Lil and I went into the motel to freshen up for supper . . . and a superb supper it was, with breaded and browned fillets accompanied by small buttered potatoes, fresh garden peas, and a crisp salad. After pie and coffee, Lil and I wandered down to the dock to watch the sunset. Pop was draped over a wooden bench, his surroundings bathed in pipe smoke.

"Fine evening," I offered.

"Aye, laddie . . . and a fine day."

I couldn't help but bring up the matter of the lures once more. "What do you think about those plastic-bodied jigs now?" I asked.

Pop pulled thoughtfully on his pipe, sent a cloud of smoke into the air, removed the pipe stem from his teeth, and aimed it at me. "Laddie, I must admit ye've got an incr-r-edible bait ther-r-e . . . an incr-r-edible bait. Had I noo been with ye I would ne'er hae believed it."

I slid onto the wooden bench alongside Pop and leaned back

with considerable inner satisfaction with the day and with having demonstrated to this hidebound old guide that modern technology was the future wave in angling.

"However-r," the old man reflected, "we could hae done a lot better-r."

"How?" I was surprised.

"Aye, laddie," he confided with certainty. "We'd hae gotten many more and much larger-r bass if we had only taken along some fr-r-ogs."

The Great Crooked Lake Bear Hunt

There probably wasn't a better location for a fishing camp than the one Billy Zup built and operated on Crooked Lake. Billy liked to say that when he came home from the U.S. Army in 1945, he took a saw and a hand ax, went up to Crooked Lake, and built the place. This, of course, was an exaggeration . . . but, then, Billy occasionally tended to exaggerate a trifle. Situated on the south shore of what was later to become part of the Boundary Waters Canoe Area and almost casting distance from the boundary of Ontario's Quetico Park, the site was surrounded by superb walleye, smallmouth bass, lake trout, and northern pike angling. It was a spot Lil and I visited almost every year, not just for the fishing, but also for the crazy things that went on up there. Billy Zup was born with a vivid imagination.

Like the summer we were up there and a Big Shot from Milwaukee was staying at the camp, one of those people who let you know he was making money faster than he could spend it. He had come to Crooked Lake looking for a trophy walleye, one he could get mounted and hang on the wall alongside all his other fish and game trophies. On earlier trips he had taken a trophy lake trout and a bass. On this venture, he managed the walleye, after a week's effort, but braced Billy at the lodge bar one night with another request.

"Zup, I'd like to get me a trophy black bear," the Big Shot said, cold beer in hand.

"This is a fishing camp . . . we don't do hunting," Billy pointed out with some diplomacy.

"Hey, come on, Zup. Suppose I come up in September. Bear season is open in September. Your camp is still open then, isn't it?"

"Yeah." Billy wiped off the varnished wood bar and uncapped a couple of cold ones. "We just never got into the bear hunting business."

"Look, Zup," the Big Shot said, jamming a finger into Billy's chest, "I want a bear rug for my living room . . . money is no object. Besides, how many times have I been up here fishing? Five? Six? I dropped several thousand bucks in your place. You could sure make room for one bear hunt, for cripes sake."

Billy rubbed his forehead. "Geez, I don't know."

"Aw, come on," the Big Shot pleaded. "It's worth five hundred for me to get a bear."

"Well, lemme think about it," Billy said. And, as he told Lil and me later, promptly forgot all about it.

But the Big Shot didn't. It was a busy summer, with dozens of anglers coming and going right up to Labor Day. The cash register was ringing, and Billy was smiling . . . until the day the Big Shot showed up again. His September reservation had come through with a bunch of bookings by anglers, but nothing further had been said about hunting; and Billy was dumbfounded when the Big Shot came into camp with camouflaged hunting clothes, two rifles, and enough ammunition to start a small war. "Ready to go bag me a bear," he announced. "And don't try to set me up with a garbage dump bear . . . I want to kill a wild one."

Nobody ever accused Billy Zup of being a slow thinker. Hoping to make the best out of a bad situation, he figured to at least make a pretense of running a hunt. At that time, Billy had a handyman working for him by the name of Kastelic, who had been a corporal in the Army during WWII. It was only natural that he should go by the name of "Corporal" Kastelic.

"Listen, Corporal," Billy said that evening. "This guy caught me by surprise. I thought he was coming up fishing, but he wants to shoot a bear. Take him around the lake in a motorboat tomorrow morning and let him look for a bear."

"I've never been bear hunting," Corporal complained. "The only bear I know about is in the garbage dump behind the camp."

"Oh, no. He made it plain he doesn't want a dump bear. Just give him a long boat ride," Billy said. "Let him enjoy the fall scenery. Maybe he'll get tired and decide to go fishing instead."

The next morning, as the lake lay shrouded in blue fall mist, Corporal had the hunter fitted into the bow of a Lund fishing boat cutting a wake through slick, still water. A few loons, gathering to migrate south, called mournfully. As the sun burned off the mist, shoreline hardwoods appeared brilliant red and yellow against dark green spruce, fir, and pine. The hunter saw ducks, beaver, muskrats, blue herons, and even a deer drinking in the shallows, but no bear.

That evening after supper, the Big Shot exploded: "Zup, this is no way to run a bear hunt, racing around the lake in a motorboat. You got to put out bait like meat scraps or bakery goods and bring the bears in."

"I told you this was a fishing camp," Billy said. "Try it again tomorrow."

The next day, the story was the same. After a high-speed inspection of all the channels, bays, and islands up the U.S. side of fourteen-mile-long Crooked Lake, the hunter was really irritated. "What kind of a camp you running here?" he bellowed in the lodge at supper time. "I thought you guys who lived in the north woods knew something about bears. This isn't bear hunting!"

The cook came out of the kitchen and whispered to Billy at the bar, "Listen, there's a heck of a big bear coming into the garbage dump every night. Maybe we can get the loudmouth to shoot it."

"Ah . . . he fancies himself some kind of a sport. He'll never sit in the dump for a shot."

"What if we set a snare and caught the bear by one foot and had it anchored to a tree? If the guy was in the woods and couldn't see the dump, how'd he know?"

"Might work," Billy agreed. "Get Corporal to help you set a snare, and maybe we can get the guy in there for a shot before it's light enough to see the cans and bottles."

As was his usual schedule, Billy was up well before daylight and came into the kitchen. Corporal was sitting disconsolate at a table, coffee mug in hand, while the cook shuffled around starting breakfast.

"Miss him?" Billy asked.

"We snared the bear, all right," the cooks said, "but we got a problem."

"What's that?"

"Instead of his foot, the bear stuck his head in the snare, and it got him around the neck. He's dead."

"Wait a minute," Bill said. "Is the bear stiff?"

"Stiff as a pine plank," Kastelic groaned.

"Well, listen." Billy stroked his chin. "Go get the boat, load the bear in, and haul him to the brushy point across the bay. Prop him up behind a log so he's standing." He paused and went on. "After breakfast, take the guy around a couple of bays in the boat, Corporal, then swing past the point and let him shoot the bear."

"Shoot the dead bear?"

"Yeah, set it up so it will fall over when the slug hits."

"O.K." Kastelic brightened up. "Geez, it might work."

The Big Shot was in a foul mood when he came down to breakfast. He complained ever more loudly about the hunting, the guide, and anything else that a crossed his mind. "This is the limit," he announced. "If we don't see anything today, I'm pulling out for Milwaukee . . . and I'm not paying one dime for this circus."

He slunk down to the boat, climbed in with an air of resignation, and settled back against a couple of boat cushions. Kastelic kicked the throttle open and they roared up the lake, the sound of the outboard still discernible long after they were swallowed up in the mist. As he had on the previous days, Kastelic cruised the shoreline, in and out of the bays, shading his eyes with one hand as the sun came over the trees and burned off the fog. Suddenly he cut the throttle and the boat coasted to a stop. "There," he whispered, pointing. "There he is."

"Where?" said the Big Shot, suddenly wide awake.

"Right there . . . up on the ridge . . . peeking over that fallen tree."

"Oh, geez . . . " the hunter fumbled to get his gun out of the leather case. "Oh, geez . . . " His hands were shaking as he jammed a clip into the magazine, jacked a shell into the chamber, and slipped off the safety.

"Take your time," Kastelic whispered. "You've got lots of time."

The Big Shot eventually got the sights centered on the bear's shoulder, cracked off a shot, and the bear vanished.

"You got him!" Kastelic yelled. "What a shot! You nailed him!"

"I did? I thought maybe I missed him. He's gone."

"Naw, he's down," Kastelic yelled, starting the motor and heading for the resort.

"Hey, what're you doing?" the Big Shot screamed. "We gotta go get that bear."

"Omigod, no!" Kastelic yelled back. "We never go right

131

in . . . just in case the bear isn't dead yet . . . it takes them a little time to die, and if you get within reach, he'd tear your head off."

"No kidding?" The Big Shot seemed suitably impressed.

"Yeah . . . I'll come back in a little bit with some more help, make sure he's dead, and haul him out."

Back at the camp, the word quickly spread around that the Big Shot had bagged his bear. Billy and a number of fishermen gathered to shake his hand and congratulate him.

The Big Shot was nervous, however, and kept looking out across the bay. "Don't you think somebody oughta go over there and make sure I got him?"

"Oh, you got him all right," Kastelic said. "I saw it. It was a heck of a shot!"

An hour went by, and Kastelic came down to the dock with one of the fishing guides. "O.K.," Kastelic said. "He should be stiffened up by now. Let's go bring him in."

The Big Shot stood in the bow of the boat, gripping the gunwales with excitement as they pulled into shore. The minute the boat hit gravel, he vaulted over the side and ran headlong up the bank.

"Look out!" Kastelic yelled. "Keep your rifle ready just in case."

The Big Shot slammed on the brakes, checked his rifle to make sure there was a shell in the chamber, then stalked carefully up to the edge of the woods.

"Wow!" he yelled down. "Wow . . . look at him! He's a whopper!"

Kastelic and the guide came up and looked at the bear, lying on the far side of the log, legs sticking out rigidly. Only now there was a bullet hole through the left shoulder. Fortunately, the Big Shot was so excited, he didn't notice there wasn't any blood oozing out of the hole. All he could see was the bear rug in front of the fireplace back home.

The hunting party returned in triumph, winched the bear up in the boat house by a back leg, and Kastelic proceeded to skin it.

The Big Shot was up at the bar the rest of the day buying round after round of drinks, embellishing the story slightly with details on how he spotted the bear sneaking along the rim of the forest, coolly laid the sights in on the bruin, and knocked him dead.

The hide went into the freezer and from there to a taxidermist in Duluth, who rendered it into a fine trophy rug with the head attached, mouth agape with a fierce expression. Billy got well paid for the expedition, and Kastelic got a hundred-dollar tip in addition to his guide's wages.

But that was the last bear shot at Zup's resort. In subsequent years we heard several fishermen query Bill about coming back up in the fall to hunt bears. Billy always shook his head. "No, we don't do bear hunts."

"Nope," echoed Corporal Kastelic. "We tried it once. Too darn dangerous."

Nuts of Neverhunt

When an old hunting dog dies, there is a time for grieving, a time for remembrance. And, eventually, there comes a time to think of another dog. Thus, some months after our old retriever Babe died, I started glancing through the outdoor magazines, studying various breeds, talking to dog-owning friends, figuring, comparing. Should I get another retriever? Or maybe a pointing dog? Tough decision.

A couple of times I had hunted woodcock and grouse with Pete Doran, owner of some very fine pointing Brittany spaniels. And some local hunters had German shorthairs with impressive credentials on both grouse and waterfowl.

I guessed, maybe, what with duck limits scaled back, perhaps a pointing dog with secondary retrieving characteristics might be a wise choice. On the other hand, Lil announced that she wasn't all that interested in another sporting breed. She noted that her friend Betty, over on the Moose Lake Road, had a miniature poodle, a blonde, cuddly wisp of a dog, which would affectionately curl up on a person's lap. In the midst of this controversy, our daughter Barb drove up from Duluth one October afternoon, just before my birthday, ending all speculation. She got out of her car with a tiny bundle of black fuzz cradled up in her arms.

"Happy birthday, Dad," she beamed, handing over the black fuzzbundle.

"What is it?" I inquired, pangs of doubt beginning to set in.

"A cockapoo."

"A what?"

"A cockapoo . . . half cocker spaniel, half poodle. They are very fine dogs, don't grow very big, and don't shed."

The doubt began to escalate into panic. "What I was looking for was a new hunting dog," I mumbled, holding the fuzzbundle up and inspecting it closely. From somewhere in the dense black foliage a pink tongue emerged and gave my fingers a tentative lick.

"Oh, look. He loves you," Barb said.

"Well, geez . . . I don't know . . . "

At this point Lil came out of the house. "Ooh, let me hold him!" She plucked fuzzy out of my hands and cuddled him close. "He's so cute . . . is he ours?"

"I got him for Dad for his birthday," Barb said.

"Oh, how nice."

The panic had now become a dull ache. How do you give a birthday present back to your daughter? But then, I rationalized, defeat might not be utter. Several cocker spaniels I had known were accomplished upland dogs. Small, yes, but eager hunters. And in Europe, I recalled from some source, poodles were used as hunting dogs. No matter what the fuzzbundle looked like, I thought, it might have the attributes of a hunter . . . and with some guidance, training, and perhaps help from God . . . who knows . . .

"He's going to be a great buddy," my wife cooed, hugging the little beast. "In fact, that's a good name for him—Buddy."

Thus it was that Buddy moved into our lives and took over our home as fall merged into winter. By spring, he began assuming the shape of a dog, with stature about that of a springer spaniel, albeit a rather hairy one. As soon as the snow left, I began tentatively working him outside with a rubber ball. He had a natural propensity for retrieving, I noted with some satisfaction, racing to pick up the ball and racing back. As spring edged toward summer, we eventually graduated to a duck-sized dummy, which he handled with a fair amount of competence.

The name Buddy, however, did not seem an appropriate appellation for a stalwart beast of the chase. One of my early retrievers, a grandson of the legendary Labrador dual champion Shed of Arden and an incredible duck and pheasant dog, had been named "Cary's Tar of Glenwood." The most recent was "Babe of Plainfield." By comparison, "Buddy" seemed a rather inadequate title.

Our neighbor Al Ito came over one day with a half dozen tomato plants for my garden. Over a period of weeks, he had observed Buddy with considerable skepticism as to the dog's possible hunting capabilities. On this day he paused to witness our exercises impassively.

"Watch," I said, hoping to impress Al with Buddy's newly developed skills. With that I hurled the dummy across the driveway to the edge of the woods and yelled, "Fetch!"

On cue, the dog tore out on a dead run. He snapped up the dummy with style, reversed field, and came trotting back, head high. Unfortunately, at that precise moment, he spotted a white cabbage butterfly sunning itself on the driveway, promptly dropped the dummy, and pointed the insect.

Al's naturally narrow eyes vanished into slits as he doubled over with mirth. Barely able to speak, he gasped, "Hoo, boy . . . that dog is nuts . . . he'll never hunt."

"Never hunt? Nuts?" Something clicked in our minds, and after a good laugh, we gave fuzzbundle a new designation: "Nuts of Neverhunt." Secretly, however, I was determined to turn this beast into a hunter, if for no other reason than to prove Al wrong.

Nuts did not readily get the training he deserved. There were too many distractions that summer. For one thing, the garden exploded with all manner of savory fare, including Al's tomatoes. For another, the smallmouth bass were on a rampage, and a lot of spare time was spent paddling the bays and points where these pugnacious warriors held forth. But at least once each week, Nuts and I had a refresher with the dummy; thus, as September moved into October, Nuts's first birthday and the waterfowl season came upon us simultaneously.

Opening day, Al, Lil, Nuts, and I were on Basswood Lake hunkered down in a point blind made of rush and scrub alder. A few distant wedges of waterfowl trailed from the wild rice paddies at the mouth of Hula Creek to the open expanse of the lake and the Ontario border beyond. A mild breeze kept our two dozen decoys shifting satisfactorily on the riffled surface, but nothing came our way. A half hour after legal shooting time, Al sighed and pulled out his thermos and three cups for one last round of coffee.

"Look out!" Lil hissed as Al barely got the cap unscrewed. "On the right!"

From the rice beds, a quartet of mallards had veered our way on slow, steady wingbeats.

Al hastily put down the Thermos, his right hand sliding toward his Browning 12-gauge leaning against the front of the blind. Lil and I both had our Remington pumps in hand.

"They're not coming in, they're going over," I muttered, watching the deliberate rhythm of the beating pinions. "Take 'em the first time by."

The ducks, at twenty-five yards altitude, were not in a decoying mood, but were curious enough to give our spread a cursory look.

The three of us came up in one motion and the mallards flared, towering straight overhead. In the ensuing fusillade, Al dropped a greenhead to the left, Lil staggered a second drake, and I finished it off as it started to glide away. The other two ducks, unscathed, powered high and wide for Canada.

"Not particularly great shooting," was Al's comment.

"Well, it's early in the year," I rationalized, climbing out of the blind with Nuts leaping up and down, eager to join in the activity. I walked out on a grassy stretch of shore, aimed my arm toward the downed ducks and yelled, "Fetch!"

Like a shot he headed for the lake, splashed into the water up to his ankles, stopped short, and stepped back out. Then he ran up and down the bank barking loudly at the two dead birds bobbing on the waves.

"Fetch," I repeated, with considerable irritation. Nuts again ran to the water's edge, jumped up and down, barked, and sat down.

Lil was giggling and Al was bent over with laughter. "Oh, you've got a retriever all right!" he howled. "You've got a retriever that can't swim!" Tears were coursing down his cheeks.

In sickening realization, I recalled that all our brief training sessions in the summer had been in the backyard on dry land. It had never occurred to me that the dog couldn't swim. I remembered he had drunk from the lake on occasional fishing trips, but he had never gone in. A few more bellowed orders to "fetch!" generated no response. In a mix of rising anger and humiliation, I strode to where our canoe was cached in the alders, pushed it into the water, grabbed a paddle, and prepared to embark. At the last moment, Nuts leaped past me, over the right gunwale, scrambled forward, and positioned himself in the bow. As I grimly paddled toward the first drake, Nuts barked enthusiastically as though urging me on. Developing a slow burn, I sculled the canoe alongside the duck, but before I could pick it up, Nuts leaned over, grabbed the bird by the neck, trotted back to the stern seat, and dropped it in my lap. He did the same with the second bird.

On the shore, Al was in stitches. "Whooee!" he chortled. "Who's the retriever? You or the dog?"

We managed two more ducks that day, but no amount of threats

139

or cajoling would convince Nuts to enter the water. He simply would not swim.

The following summer, both Lil and I tried without success to get him into the lake. We even took him out in the canoe and deliberately swamped the craft. Instead of swimming for shore, he circled frantically, crying piteously.

"He just can't swim," Lil concluded, helping him back to the bank.

It was something that we had to accept. He was a nice, friendly house dog and did a fair job of shagging woodchucks out of the garden, but was not worth much afield. We even tried him on grouse, but his main contribution there was to bolt ahead on a dead run into the coverts and flush the birds well out of range.

One golden autumn evening, Nuts and I sat on the back porch holding a discussion while I trimmed and pared a mess of carrots for supper. "Some of your ancestors may have been hunting dogs," I said, "but it was so many generations back, it must have gotten bred clean out of your genes."

The dog raised one eyebrow, brought a hind leg forward, and scratched his ear.

"You were a birthday gift," I continued, "and you can live here as long as you wish, but a hunting dog you are not."

Lil came out on the back porch and picked up the carrots. Nuts followed her back inside. The woods were illuminated by one of those gorgeous fall sunsets, with the maples flaming yellow and scarlet, the birch a rustling mass of shimmering gold. I had started spreading straw over the rhubarb plants when a movement in the hazel brush alongside the garden caught my attention. The crested head of a cock grouse poked up, peering at me with unblinking, beady eyes.

"Ho!" I said softly. "Here's a fowl to go with the carrots."

Careful not to alarm the bird, I backed away slowly, then hurried up the back steps and into the house. In the living room, I grabbed my shotgun off the rack and a picked a pair of shells from the drawer.

"What's up?" Lil inquired.

"Grouse. Out by the garden."

I hustled to the back door, but with my attention fixed on the bird, I forgot about the dog. He had watched me take down the gun, and as I opened the door to go out, he darted past me. The grouse was now out in the open, crossing the driveway in plain view. With a yip, Nuts dashed for it.

"Whoa! Whup! Stop!" My shouts were to no avail. The grouse bolted into the forest understory, Nuts hot after him. Calling all manner of curses on the dog, I sprinted up the drive, stopped, and peered into the shadowy jumble of alder, hazel brush, and balsam.

Oddly enough, the grouse hadn't flushed, even with the dog in hot pursuit, and I began to think it had simply run off into the woods. Then I made out the black form of Nuts, anchored on three feet, one paw raised, muzzle thrust forward.

For a split second I was dumbfounded. He was definitely on point, but what was he pointing? I eased forward. "Steady, boy," I murmured. He quivered but kept his stance. In a thunder of wings, the bird came out almost under my feet, curved over the brush, shaved a balsam, and rocketed straight for a birch clump. I swung with the vanishing target, squeezing the trigger. At the crash, the bird dropped in a puff of grayish brown feathers.

"Hot dang!" I shucked the empty shell out of the magazine and started forward, only to see the hazel brush shaking violently. I heard a faint "wuff! wuff!" and out of the thicket came Nuts, the bird clamped solidly in his jaws. It would be nice to report that he finished with a classic retrieve, but he didn't. He came within six feet, dropped the bird, sat down, and proceeded to cough and spit loose feathers from his mouth. But he had performed admirably. I hefted the grouse, then knelt down by the dog and stroked his head. "You did it, Nuts," I murmured. "You pointed and you retrieved."

"Wuff! Wuff!" he said, tail wagging wildly.

It would also be nice to report that Nuts thenceforth became a great pointer, but he didn't do that, either. In twelve succeeding years, he has never pointed another bird. Now he is getting old and gray, gimpy with arthritis in his hind legs. But once, just once on a glorious autumn evening, when the trees were a blaze of color, some long-lost instinct from his ancient heritage took control of that cockapoo and he registered a classic point. For those few brief moments, Nuts of Neverhunt became a bird dog.

Hustled on the Mitawan

Mike Banovetz, at age eighteen, was a dedicated stream trout angler. He is still a dedicated stream trout angler, but not like when he was eighteen. Maybe "dedicated" is a poor description. A better word might be "fanatic." When he worked as a wilderness guide for Lil and me at our canoe outfitting base on Moose Lake, he talked about trout fishing nonstop. When he had a few hours or a day off, he went trout fishing. Due to time constraints, his range was somewhat limited to the series of small, cold, clear streams that flow north from the Laurentian Divide into the Isabella River, thence to the Minnesota-Ontario border waters, and continuing west and north to Hudson Bay.

The overall geography was certainly less than a major concern to Mike. His focus was entirely on the fish. These small, north-flowing streams get relatively little attention from most of the trout-fishing establishment. Those worthy folk tend to concentrate on better-known rivers and creeks that flow south from the Laurentian Divide into Lake Superior and thence to the Atlantic Ocean. Substantial streams like the Cascade, Temperance, Knife, Baptism, and Poplar.

The Isabella River tributaries have almost unknown names like Inga, Arrowhead, Jack, Dumbbell, and Mitawan. It was adjacent to this last stream that we parked the company pickup truck at midday on a fine, sunshiny Saturday in June. We were on a logging road near a bridge where Forest Road 173 spans the narrow stream, and we were eating lunch.

An uncharacteristic lull in the outfitting business that day had given us the afternoon and evening off. Uncharacteristic in the summer, because canoe trip outfitting is normally a sixteen-hour-a-day, seven-day-a-week enterprise. Mike was a wilderness canoe guide and usually on the water, but this Saturday was a rare day off between trips. A day for trout fishing.

The Mitawan, like the others nearby, is small by any standard, but it is spring fed, riffling over gleaming gravel bars, curling under streamside alders and willows, and eddying into shadowy pools that harbor brook trout that run anywhere from six inches to a foot or more in length. There are, it should be noted, very few of those foot-long specimens. The average is eight or nine inches. A thirteen-incher is a trophy. But what handsome, native fish they are— and were. A species surviving from glacial times, undiluted with hatchery rearlings. Scarlet-finned, brilliantly spotted, olive-backed with creamy squiggles, they are deep red inside and tasty when fried up golden brown in butter. Our aim, on such rare jaunts as this, was to procure enough of these small fish for a trout fry when we got back home. The limit was ten per person.

Mike and I were leaning on the hood of the truck, jamming down sandwiches from our bag lunches and plotting the afternoon strategy. "I think . . . I will fish . . . the pools . . . downstream," Mike announced between bites.

"Fine. Then I'll go upstream," I said.

It was not that I disliked his companionship. It was just that we had incompatible angling methods. My modus operandi consisted of moving along at a leisurely pace, studying the pools carefully to determine if there was a means of approaching them in such a way that a fly could be cast into an opening, no matter how small. The problem was that the Mitawan was densely rimmed with spruce, birch, popple, willow, and alder brush. It was extremely difficult to locate a casting site where the back cast would not wind up snagged in the foliage, not to mention an errant forward cast in which the leader might wrap itself around an overhanging branch, the fly dangling carefree in the wind.

Much of my time was taken up retrieving the fly from various parts of the understory. Sometimes it was merely a matter of bending a limb down to free the barb, but other embarrassing instances required clambering up a tree trunk and severing the offending branch with my pocketknife to get the leader and fly back to earth.

Mike, on the other hand, used a completely different, rather unique, approach. No thoughtful, carefully planned stalk for him. He crashed through the brush or plowed down the current like a bull moose in rut. In a sense, he stormed a stream, intent on decimating the trout population as quickly and efficiently as possible. He was armed with a can of worms, a bag to put the fish in, an old steel fly rod that telescoped down to three feet in length, and a reel with ten-pound-test monofilament, a size eight hook tied on the terminal end.

When he came within range of any segment of stream he thought might harbor a trout, he baited up with a worm, jammed the telescoping rod through an opening in the brush, and extended it section by section, until the worm hovered over the water. Then he released a foot or two of line and let the bait fall into the stream and go about its work. If he got snagged up, he simple reefed in on the ten-pound-test line until the hook ripped free from the brush. He did not like to use a lighter line, that might break. Mike felt tying on another hook wasted good fishing time, not to mention hooks. Bait time in the water was critical.

If he detected a strike, he would narrow his eyes, clench his jaw, lean forward slightly, then set the hook with his left hand as hard and abruptly as circumstances would allow. While other, more orthodox, trout anglers might at this point have savored the battle with a surging brookie, Mike concentrated on the immediate harvest. The second the fish was on the hook, he stripped in both the line and the telescoping rod, dragging his thrashing prize through brush and grass to where he stood. The moment his fingers closed down on the slippery trout, he emitted a satisfied "Ah-hah!," bagged the fish, and crashed on a dead run through the brush to the next pool to repeat the process.

Between the loud crashes and an occasional "Ah hah!," it was possible to trace his progress until the noise vanished in the distance. In a good afternoon, Mike would take the ten-trout limit in perhaps a half mile of brush crashing, clattering back hours later with a broad smile of success. At no time can I recall an instance when anyone else caught more trout quicker than Mike. While his methods and tackle were not exactly the stuff of fine sportsmanship, his dexterity and aptitude were beyond question. They were matched by sharply focused, single-minded pursuit.

Once, I was told, he went fishing with an elderly trout angler of some reputation, a more traditional type such as one might see in an L.L. Bean catalog illustration or in *Field and Stream* magazine. He was a person imbued with the poetry of moving water, the lushness of the scenery, the myriad bird life. At the end of the day, while inspecting Mike's bag full of eight-to-ten-inchers, the gentleman noted that he had caught and released a half dozen trout, one of which he estimated to be in excess of twelve inches.

"Excuse me?" Mike said, incredulously.

"Catch-and-release," the gentleman said with modest pride. "I released them all unharmed."

"Never went fishing with that guy again," Mike was said to have stated with undisguised disgust.

The sole purpose of fishing, Mike regularly affirmed, was to catch fish to eat. The sport was in how fast this could be accomplished. There was a secondary amount of excitement, of course, when the fish were browned in hot butter and subsequently devoured.

In any event, on this gorgeous June day, we were just finishing up our sandwiches when an ancient pickup truck, equipped with a tank and aerator, drove into view. It came to halt in a small cloud of dust, and from behind the wheel emerged the smiling, gray-haired Bait Lady. This legendary personage operated a combined store, gas station, and live bait emporium on Highway One, in the tiny community of Isabella. She eyed us for a moment, dusted her hands on her blue jeans, and inquired, "Goin' fishin', boys?"

"That's right," I replied. Mike mumbled something unintelligible through a mouthful of sandwich.

Most anglers knew this lady by sight and reputation. She not only sold them worms, minnows, sandwich supplies, and cold pop, she was also a source of information on local trout angling. And she was rated as one of the most skillful trout prospectors between the Isabella River and the North Shore of Lake Superior. Indeed, if one might gain her confidence, she could be induced to crack open her freezer for a peek at whatever manner of trout she had recently conquered. These were inevitably of impressive dimensions, usually in the fourteen-inch or better category, real eye-poppers for those of us accustomed to somewhat smaller fare.

These fish, she invariably pointed out, came from the Little Isabella River, a scenic but hard-fished stream with a well-developed Forest Service campground nearby. We were well aware that the fish in the freezer did not come from the Little Isabella, and we were sure she knew that we knew. But angling etiquette required that we merely nod and remark on the quality of her catch.

When she did her fishing was a matter of considerable speculation. Since she spent a lot of time tending the store or running her minnow traps, we believe that perhaps she ventured forth before daylight or after dark. Neither Mike, nor I, nor any of our angling fraternity, ever saw her fishing. But she did have the irrefutable proof in her freezer. Thus, when we met her at this particular section of the Mitawan, our interest immediately jumped up a few notches. Was this, we thought, one of those places where she captured those trophy trout?

However, she appeared to have no fishing equipment with her. In rubber knee boots she strode over to the stream and lifted a min-now trap from beneath the bridge. Its wiggling, silvery contents were dumped into a plastic bucket and transferred to the aerated minnow tank on the back of her truck. That done, she came over and leaned her elbows on the hood of my pickup.

"Where are you planning to seek your luck?" she inquired.

Mike by now had swallowed all of his bread and peanut butter. "Downstream, from the bridge," he confided.

"I'm going the other way," I said.

"Fair number of fish in this stretch," she agreed, "but mainly small. If you want the big trout, the twelve-to-fourteen-inchers, you've got to hike back to where the beaver dams start."

"What beaver dams?" Mike asked.

"Over there." She waved a hand upstream.

"We didn't know about those," I confessed.

"Hardly anybody does," she replied. "Too tough to get back in there . . . but that's where the big ones are."

I pulled out a wrinkled U.S. Forest Service map and spread it on the truck hood. She ran a gnarled finger from where we were into an area south and west. "Don't ever tell anyone about this," she whispered, her blue eyes gleaming in a conspiratorial manner. "There is an old game trail that follows the stream, then veers off. You have to look sharp to find the trail, but it leads straight to the first beaver dam. The others are above there." She paused for a moment, running a hand through her silvery hair. "If you've got what it takes, that's where you'll find 'em, but don't breathe a word to anyone, for heaven's sake."

"Heck no, we wouldn't tell anyone," Mike said quickly.

We thanked her for this vital bit of information as she slid back behind the wheel of her pickup, waved, and drove away.

"Wow!" Mike said. "Let's get going."

His enthusiasm was contagious, and with high anticipation and a thick layer of mosquito repellant, we dove into the streamside brush and began our quest for the brook trout Holy Grail. Within a short distance, we came upon the game trail, with hoof marks indicating it was used quite frequently by a family of moose. For a time we could hear the stream gurgling on our left. And occasionally we caught a quick glimpse of blue water shimmering in the sunlight. We were tempted to pause and try our luck, but the lure of distant beaver dams and trophy trout kept us moving ahead. Unfortunately, the game trail began to peter out, and the going got infinitely more difficult. Still, we crashed ahead through alder thickets and patches of saw grass that seemed intent on shredding our pants.

After more than an hour, we stopped to mop our faces and lather on a new application of mosquito repellent. It was apparent that the resident insects back in this swampy locale were bordering on a state of desperate starvation. The sun was still high overhead, the wind negligible, and the heat oppressive. Still, we labored on toward the beaver dams. Eventually we emerged from the brush on the edge of a vast bog. The stream had dwindled to a series of trickles, which we could follow only by hopping from one grassy hummock to another. Between the hummocks, we found to our dismay, lay a type of soft, wet muck usually referred to locally as "loon doo-doo."

"Whoa, Mike!" I gasped out at last.

"What?"

"Whoa. Where do you think you're going?"

"To find the beaver dams."

"Mike, my lad," I sighed, "there are no beaver dams."

"Whatta you mean . . . the lady said . . . "

"I know what the lady said. But look around. We are in the middle of a vast bog. There is no longer any trout stream. There is nothing but acres and acres of grass. There are not even any alders or willows if a beaver wanted to build a dam."

Mike stared around, dazed. He wipe his sweaty face in disbelief. "But she said . . . "

"Ah, yes, she said . . . " I flicked a trickle of perspiration from my nose. "Mike, we were too close to some of her favorite trout pools. She sent us off into this no-man's-land to get us away from there."

"You mean she lied to us?"

"Let us say she engaged in a certain amount of deception."

Mike let out a roar of profanity, surprisingly extensive for a young man of eighteen years. "Well, I'll tell you what," he snarled, somewhat regaining his composure. "The next time I see her pickup truck parked by one of those bridges where she's got minnow traps, I'm gonna take my fillet knife and slash her tires."

"Hold it," I said. "Look at the big picture. You and I have just been witness to a superb performance. Notice how she leaned her elbows on the truck hood, let the wind stir a few gray locks of hair, and stared at us with those innocent blue eyes . . .and then told us in exact detail where those nonexistent beaver dams were located."

"Yeah, but . . . "

"No buts. With fishing, like love and war, all's fair. As you go through life, young man, you may, from time to time, encounter anglers who have developed deceit to the level of art. Back there by the bridge, we were privileged to view an incredible performance."

"We got taken by that old lady's blue eyes."

"Yeah, true. But recall how skillfully and how cleverly it was done . . . with such conviction."

"I think we ought go right over to her store and chew her out."

"Oh, no, Mike. That would only confirm that her hoax had been an eminent success. Besides, there is some daylight left. Let us retrace our steps and see if we can come up with a few trout from the pools above and below the bridge . . . and take care of this little problem later."

"Get even?"

"Yes, but not in any physical sense."

We did manage to take eight fat little eight-to-nine-inch trout before dark, certainly no bonanza, but a worthwhile evening considering our rather weary and disheveled condition. As we started back in the dark, Mike inquired, "You going over there and give her what for?"

"No," I said. "She could tell just by looking at our beat-up appearance that we took the bait. But tomorrow I have to drive down Highway One to the North Shore. Refreshed and cleanly clothed, I will stop in at her bait shop, order a cold bottle of pop, toss a few coins on the counter, and tell that nice old lady that we got our limits of trout with a couple over thirteen inches. I will tell her we got 'em all in the pools above and below the bridge . . . just didn't figure we had time to go looking for those beaver dams . . . but thanks for the tip and we intend to fish them sometime soon."

"What if she doesn't believe you?"

"Doesn't make any difference. She will never know if we did or didn't get a limit of trout on the Mitawan or if we bought her beaver dam story. She will never know if she conned us or I conned her."

"Fair enough," laughed Mike. "Let's go home and fry the fish."

The Pope and Young Bear

Larry Whitmore is a dead shot with a bow and arrow. Within twenty-five yards, he can place a barbed shaft in a target with very nearly the same pinpoint accuracy as a rifle shooter. When I first met Larry, a quarter century ago, he had racked up several whitetail and mule deer, a wild turkey, and a couple of antelope with his bow. What the young man had never done was put an arrow into a trophy black bear, an experience he hankered for with almost compulsive zeal. Indeed, he talked endlessly about getting a bear that would make the record book established in the names of the legendary archers Art Young and Dr. Saxton Pope.

For several seasons, Larry had been a staff member of the Boy Scout High Adventure Canoe Base, just east of my home on the shore of Moose Lake, eighteen miles east of Ely. At that time, Lil and I owned and operated Canadian Border Outfitters, supplying equipment and food for wilderness campers heading into the federal Boundary Waters Canoe Area and Ontario's adjacent Quetico Provincial Park. When the scout base buttoned up for the summer, Larry came down the lake looking for work. It so happened some of our staff had left for college and we needed an extra hand. Larry filled the bill nicely as a guide and equipment packer.

The previous fall, I had nailed a 250-pound male bear with an arrow, a trophy that provided some tasty shoulder roasts and a thick rug in the lodge living room. It was one of six or seven taken by bow hunters at our lodge over several seasons, all of which provided an endless source of fodder for late evening hunting tales accompanied by steaming mugs of coffee.

"Sure like to get a shot at a good bear," Larry said during one of our after-hours story sessions. "How's chances this fall?"

"If you're figuring on firing an arrow into a bear," we told Larry, "you've got to pick your trails, bait 'em up, and have an infinite amount of patience. For a single, killing shot, you have to bait the bear in close . . . make the bear come to you."

Veteran archery hunters, we pointed out, agree that black bears often present difficult targets. They usually come to a bait on all fours, face-on; but a frontal shot in such cases is almost useless, since the arrow will strike little except bone. Also, bears tend to be extremely wary, hanging back in the understory, where a hasty arrow may be deflected by branches. That's where the infinite patience comes in. A rifle shooter can nail a bear as soon as the bear comes in view, but a bow hunter must play a nerve-testing waiting game, remaining motionless with bow on draw or half-draw while the bear circles, sniffs, and crunches around. Occasionally, when a bear is scouting a bait site, he will pause on the fringe of the brush and raise up on his back legs for a look, presenting an effective heart or lung shot; but usually all the hunter sees is the head. Once the animal is really committed to the bait, he may lumber into the clearing for a good side shot. And some hunters prefer tree stands, where an overhead shot can be delivered with killing accuracy.

"One thing about a bear," I added, "when hit with an arrow, he will jump in the direction he's facing and let out a spine-chilling yowl. However, bears usually run only a short distance before stopping to try and pull the razor-head from the wound with teeth or claws. That invariably finishes them off. None of the bears we have taken with bow and arrow ran more than two hundred yards."

Guide Harry Lambirth noted that among the half dozen or so bears that had recently come into the base intent on raiding our garbage cans, one was definitely of trophy size. None of these bears had much luck in our area because we kept the garbage hauled daily and our food supply shack was built extra strong and kept locked tight at night. In addition, our two dogs set up an unearthly clamor whenever a bear came around, making any black-robed invader realize he was not exactly welcome.

Larry's eyes lit up with interest when Harry mentioned the big bear he had seen. "Any chance we could lure him in for a shot?"

"Yeah . . . good chance. We've been saving some bacon rinds in the outfitting shack," Harry noted.

For canoe trips we packed slab bacon in five-pound chunks, double-smoked for us in the local meat markets. The heavily-smoked slabs, we found, not only kept better in the woods than commercially sliced bacon but were preferred by our guests. Camp breakfasts featuring slab bacon sliced thick off the rind, fried over an open fire and served up with eggs or flapjacks, were rated as a special treat. Quite often, canoeists packed out the rinds from wilderness trips, along with other leftovers. These were saved and stored in the freezer for possible bear bait.

Over the years, bears dwelling in our locality had developed a network of trails they followed habitually along the lakeshores, over the ridges, and around the swamps. A couple of these trails meandered along the rim of a big marsh a half mile from our base, and it was in this area we put out several bacon rinds. To prevent ravens, foxes, and other smaller critters from running off with the baits, we buried them in bucket-sized holes, then covered the holes with a pile of small logs. Bears visiting the baits would hurl the logs to the side and devour the rinds or haul them away. The bait sites were carefully located within easy bow range of shooting stands, usually camouflaged with brush and balsam boughs. A bait became "active" when a bear began visiting a site regularly. We replenished the bait just as regularly, piling the logs back in place. Once interested, a bear would keep returning on an almost daily basis. However, a bear did not lose his wariness and would usually circle a site, carefully testing the air currents for human scent, watching for movement, and quickly lumbering off if his suspicions were aroused. Some bait sites simply didn't work. These we abandoned, concentrating the bacon rinds on the active ones.

Two of these active sites near the swamp were getting regular attention. One was adjacent to the burned-out shell of an ancient white pine, a massive relic from a fire that raged through the forest in the 1930s. With a hollow interior adequate to accommodate an archer, the charred snag provided a natural hiding place. The bait was located about thirty feet away in a grassy depression so the hunter would be looking down on the target. The other site was where two trails crisscrossed on top of a ridge. On the east side of the crossing, in consideration of a prevailing west wind, we constructed a hideaway of brush and boughs. The bait was located next to the trail, close enough for a telling shot if the time came. Bear tracks indicated one heck of a big boar and a couple of smaller bears were regularly visiting both sites.

Hopes were high as the first dry days of autumn began changing the maples from green to orange, the sumac to purplish red, and the aspen to brownish yellow. Larry and I spent several late afternoons on watch without a shot, the bears apparently coming in after dark to take the baits. One golden evening, the second week of the season, with a hint of frost in the air, we eased quietly to our stands—Larry in the hollow pine, I on the ridge. A pair of gray jays swished down for a look as I put out a fresh bait, replaced the strewn-about logs, and settled in on a board seat behind the balsam thatch. Other than the chirp of chickadees and the distant hammer of a pileated woodpecker drilling a dead tree, there was soft, sunwashed silence. A half hour went by, and I was dozing slightly when brought sharply alert by the distinct "whung" of a bowstring in the valley below, immediately followed by the thunderous yowl of a wounded bear and two sets of crashes in the underbrush. One set of crashes went directly away; the other was coming through the forest right at me.

Assuming we had a wounded bear raging through the woods, I stepped clear of the stand, somewhat shakily nocked an arrow, and pulled my fifty-five-pound Kodiak bow to full draw. The crashing turned into a steady hammering of footsteps as the approaching creature tore out of the understory and hit the packed trail about fifty paces away. Breath stuck in my throat, I braced myself for one quick shot. Holding the bowstring tight against my cheek, I sighted down the razor point, then dropped my aim with a sigh of relief as Larry broke into the clearing, wild-eyed and sprinting like the devil was on his heels. He looked like he was going to run right past me, so I grabbed him by the shirt.

"Did you hit him?" I yelled in his face. However, his feet kept churning, causing us to whirl around in a chaotic dance.

"Outta here!" Larry gasped, trying to jerk loose. "We gotta get outta here!"

"Wait a minute!" I yelled, still hanging on. "Did you hit him?"

"Omigod! A monster! Like King Kong!" He tried to pull free from my grip. "We gotta get outta here!"

We waltzed around a few more times, the pace slowing somewhat; then, out of breath, we stopped. There was no sound of pursuit in the forest. I let go of his shirt.

"Omigod!" he blurted. "A monster. It charged right at me."

Between wheezes and frequent wary glances down his back trail, Larry choked his story out. The huge bear had stalked arrogantly to the bait and hurled the logs aside, and was reaching for the bacon rind when Larry leaned out of the hollow pine and fired an arrow between the bear's shoulder blades. At the impact, the startled bruin roared up, claws flailing, and leaped toward the hollow pine. Larry promptly leaped the other way, shifted into overdrive, and crashed though the woods until he hit the trail where we met.

Pointing out that bears invariably jump the way they are facing when hit, I assured Larry the beast was not after him. "Listen . . . he would have had you within two jumps if he was really after you," I said.

"Oh yeah?" he countered. "Well, I was there. You weren't."

"Look, if you shot him down between the shoulder blades, you probably hit the lungs or the heart. It's a good bet he's dead by now."

"Oh yeah . . . and maybe he's not!"

"Betcha he's down. At least we've got to go back for a look."

"Geez, I don't know." Larry looked around nervously. "Why don't we come back later?"

"It won't hurt to look."

"What if he's just wounded and mad?"

"We shoot him again."

Larry was far from convinced, but we started back down the trail, bows ready, heading for the hollow pine. Larry's eyes kept darting from left to right, as though momentarily expecting the bear to come raging out of the underbrush at us.

At the bait site there were claw marks where the bear ripped the turf, but no blood. "Sure you got a hit on him?" I asked in a low voice.

"I saw the arrow go between his shoulder blades . . . right up to the fletching."

Great
Material on
the web

other Stones!

"Well, he's got to be here some place. I'll hunt for his tracks . . . you keep a sharp eye for any movement ahead."

"Don't worry." Larry's knuckles were white where he gripped his bow.

On hands and knees I began hunting for scuff marks on the forest duff. It was tough, slow tracking, but where the bear had gone under some overhanging hazel brush there was a bright patch of red.

"He's leaking out the top," I whispered. "The arrow didn't go clear through . . . it must be buried inside him."

"You can believe it," Larry whispered back, his eyes flickering warily from side to side.

The sun was slanting down and the forest turning shadowy. It was imperative to find and dress out that bear before dark. If left overnight, the hide could be ruined.

The tracks angled downhill, eventually coming out on a worn, somewhat muddy game trail that rimmed the swamp. For a hundred yards the claw marks were easier to follow, but then suddenly vanished. Dropping back, I left my cap as a marker at the last set of tracks and began circling around.

"What's wrong?" Larry asked, nervously.

"Lost him." I said. "Lost his tracks."

"Did he go into the swamp?"

That was a thought. On my knees I inspected the dense wall of tall swamp grass towering higher than my head. Where the grass was bent inward, a spot of scarlet caught my eye. And then another.

"Blood," I whispered. "He went into the swamp right here."

Still on my knees, I carefully parted the tall grass where it was bent over . . . and abruptly came face-to-face with the bear, huge mouth wide open, teeth bared, eyes glaring. In a panic, I did a desperate back flip worthy of Olympic competition, landed on my feet, and dashed up alongside Larry, who had his bow at full draw. Fortunately, there was no sound of pursuit.

"Did you see him?" Larry whispered hoarsely.

"See him? Geez, I almost crawled down his throat," I gasped.

"He didn't move?"

"Nope . . . but he was looking right at me."

After a minute, and hearing no sound, I very cautiously tiptoed back to the edge of the swamp and peered over the bent grass. A few feet in, I made out the inert black, furry form. I yelled, "Hey!" but there was no movement. I poked the bear with the tip of my bow. The massive black form stayed put.

Then I parted the grass cautiously, bringing the huge head into view. Although it stared wide-eyed, mouth open and teeth glistening, it was apparent that the bear was dead. Seriously hit, the big boar had lumbered into the edge of the swamp, climbed over a fallen log, turned to face his pursuers, and simply expired. But instead of his head hitting the ground, his jaw came to rest on the log, which propped it up even with my line of vision when I was on my knees. Even dead, the big carnivore appeared fearsome.

Larry edged up, bow ready. "I told you it was a monster," he affirmed, taking in the huge, thickly furred bulk.

By far, it was the biggest ever seen in our area, an immense male. It was so big the two of us couldn't budge it. We obviously had to get it out of the swamp to dress it, so we hiked back to the canoe base and returned in our four-wheel-drive van with Lil and staff members Harry and Mary Lambirth and Pat Flannery. We also brought a chain saw and a one-inch hemp rope. With all of us tugging, we pulled the bear from the swamp to the adjacent trail, where we could dress him out. Still, the six of us could drag him only with extreme difficulty, and it was four hundred yards to the road.

With the chain saw and a lot of heavy work, we cleared out enough of a trail through the woods to back in the four-wheeler.

We skidded the bear, roped by the neck, to the edge of the road, where we tugged and levered him onto the tailgate of the van.

It took Harry and Larry half the night to get the huge mammal skinned out. Dressed, it weighed 480 pounds. Not all in one piece, however. We didn't have a scale that would register that much. We weighed all the pieces, the head and the hide, then added them together. In the rough, that bruin must have gone between 550 and 600 pounds. Larry took the head and hide down to a taxidermist in Duluth to get a mount made. Noting that the green skull measured well over the seventeen points required for entry into the Pope and Young record book, Larry had the taxidermist set it aside to dry.

Winter came, and Larry left for his home in the west. It was almost a year before I saw him again. "How did the bear come out?" I asked.

"The mount came out great," Larry said somewhat soberly, "but somebody swiped the skull."

"What?"

"Honest. The taxidermist was really embarrassed . . . said he never had anything like that happen before. Somehow, somebody spotted that big skull and swiped it off the shelf."

"Geez, that's awful," I sympathized.

"Yeah. Well, my trophy bear is probably in the Pope and Young record book but it isn't under the name of Larry Whitmore . . . it's under the name of somebody who never shot it."

And Larry's bear became one more legend of the north woods we love to tell late at night over mugs of steaming coffee.

Playing It Close

"Four P.M." Harry Lambirth checked his wristwatch. "Magie ought to be flying in here by five or so."

We were stretched out on the grassy shore of Fourtown Lake—Harry, his wife, Mary, Lil, and I, resting our backs after paddling and portaging in from Crooked Lake. We had come up the Horse River, crossed Horse Lake and the portage to Fourtown, then paddled to the clearing on the west shore where back in the 1920s the old Cloquet rail line brought locomotives in to pick up massive white pine logs. The huge pines were long gone and the railroad with them, but parts of the old rail bed remained, designated as U.S. Forest Road 1036, which twisted fifteen miles north from the sawmill town of Winton past Cedar Lake, Low Lake, Range River, and Mudro Lake. From there to Fourtown the road was abandoned, but the forest growth had yet to reclaim it. In the early 1970s, this area was still outside the Boundary Waters Wilderness and accessible by float plane.

Legendary Minnesota bush pilot and flight instructor Pat Magie (now a legend in Alaska) had flown us to Fourtown Lake with an agreement to pick us up in the afternoon eight days later. It had been a bright, warm week, the October sun highlighting the gold, orange, and blazing red of hardwood foliage and putting a warm glow on the bright green needles of spruce, fir, and pine. Like canoe-borne Gypsies, we had simply wandered the border lakes with no particular itinerary. We sort of lived off the land from Wheelbarrow Falls down past Lower Basswood Falls to the Indian rock paintings and beyond. When we got hungry, we shot a few ducks or a few grouse, caught walleyes or bass. We had seen no other canoe campers all week. Our only neighbors were some solitary loons that continually moaned about the frosty nights, occasional beavers busy with their fall cutting, otters diving for crawfish, and eagles soaring overhead on the watch for surfacing tulibees. It had been a great trip, but time was up and we were back at the pickup point on Fourtown, along with our two canoes, packsacks, gun cases, and fishing tackle.

We shared a couple of candy bars, dozed with our backs against the packsacks, and paid little attention as fingers of haze reached across the sky from the south, turning the sun into a dull yellow blob. It was warm on shore, and the haze didn't appear storm threatening. Visibility was still more than a mile.

We were aroused by the throaty drone of the twin-engine Beechcraft coming out of the haze from the south. Magie banked the silver-and-red plane over the treeline, settled in with a shower of foam curling off the floats, then taxied to the shore and cut the power.

The cargo door on the fuselage swung open and Magie jumped down to one of the floats. "How'd it go?" he yelled, tossing us a rope.

"Great!" We looped the rope around a handy pine, warped the plane to shore, tied it off, and started sliding canoes up to him. The aircraft had been customized with an extra-wide side cargo entry so that two seventeen-foot Grumman canoes could be pushed up inside the fuselage and stacked one on top of the other. Next, we handed up Duluth packs, guns, and tackle, then untied the rope, scrambled up the pontoon to the cargo door, and climbed in.

From the pilot's seat in the front, Magie yelled back, "You got enough food left in case we have to stay out all night?"

"Sure," Harry laughed. "We've got some bacon and a little coffee left, but why the heck would we stay here tonight?"

Magie was checking the controls, reading all the gauges. "Fog bank coming in from Lake Superior. It was turning to soup when I left the base at Sandy Point and headed north."

We laughed at that one. Magie was a great kidder. The left engine choked out a puff of white exhaust, then settled into a steady roar. The right prop began to rotate, the engine coughed and took hold. Relaxed after a long day in the canoes, we settled back for the ride home. Like a great bird, the ship began gathering speed, came off the water, and soared over the shoreline trees, heading for the timbered hills to the south. Within minutes we saw what Magie had been talking about. Streamers of fog began to whip past under the wings. We approached a massive grayish white cloud bank that blotted out the sun completely. In minutes, we were flying through gusts of the stuff, the trees below disappearing and reappearing as Magie nosed the Beech lower and lower, trying to get under it. Finally, he zeroed in on the Cloquet Line, which appeared like a winding ribbon cut through the forest, but even though we were almost on the treetops, that landmark began to vanish. The four of us in the cargo hold were now sitting straight up, staring with deep concern through the windows at the scene streaking past.

With a roar of the throttle, Magie banked the Beechcraft into a sharp 180-degree turn and aimed the twin props back the way we had just come. We burst out of the fog bank and into clearer, although overcast, conditions. Next we cut 90 degrees west, the pilot seeking an opening to Burntside Lake, where he knew we could land at one of the resorts and phone for a van to come pick us up. We were roaring perhaps five hundred feet over the top of the forest, no more than two miles from the lake, when the fog bank enveloped the plane again. Another 90 degrees east, and the forest emerged dimly into view below. Visibility was fading fast, and Magie was now looking for a place to land . . . any place. Just when it seemed like the whole world was about to vanish in white, we came out over a swampy clearing. "Grassy Lake," Magie called back tersely. We were now holding our breaths and offering silent prayers as he laid the Beech over on its side and screamed around the marshy expanse, the right wingtip almost brushing the cattails. At the end of Grassy Lake a ribbon of silver appeared—the small stream flowing into adjacent Low Lake. He aimed the nose of the ship down the creek while we watched terrified as the fog blotted out the timbered hills to the right and left.

Suddenly, right under us, there was water! We breathed a sigh of relief as the pontoons leveled off about fifteen feet over the surface, and we anticipated the landing. But we didn't land!

"Drop down!" I prayed. "For heaven's sake, land it!"

Instead Magie kept roaring ahead until the dark line of trees marking the far end of Low Lake appeared out of the gloom. Horrified, we gasped as he raised the nose of the Beech and climbed into the smothering blankets of fog. Oh, Lord, I thought. We'll never find the lake again . . . why, oh why did he go back up?

Then he suddenly cut the throttle on the twin engines, and we began dropping through the white blanket. I glanced at Lil. Her jaw was set, her face grim. Harry and Mary were staring out the windows, petrified. I found myself bracing my legs, anticipating a horrendous crash into the timber. Instead, there was a split-second view of water below the floats, and we splashed in lightly, slowing as the pontoons carved twin streaks of foam in the slick, black surface. Magie cut the right motor and taxied ahead with the left. Then he cut that engine, and we coasted toward the dimly emerging shore in utter silence.

Suddenly, Magie swiveled around in the pilot's seat, his freckled face split in a wide grin: "Hey! Welcome to Bass Lake! Grab a rope and get out on the floats . . . pull us into the bank!"

In frantic relief, Harry and I scrambled for the cargo door, slid out on the right float with a coil of hemp, then eased over the side.

We looped one end of the rope to a steel cleat on the pontoon, then waded to a nearby sand strip and tugged the big craft up to where it grounded and stuck. Magie flipped us a second line and we tied off the back of the float, so the plane was tethered parallel to the shore.

"That'll hold her till morning," he said. "I'll come back tomorrow and fly 'er out. Let's get the heck out of here while we can still see a little bit." He aimed his finger toward a dim foot trail heading west. "The highway is just fifteen minutes away."

Not only was the world smothered with fog, but darkness was rapidly moving in. Lil and Mary waded ashore, grabbed two guns and two packsacks, and took off down the trail. As Harry, Magie, and I prepared to shoulder the rest of the gear, I grabbed the pilot by the sleeve.

"What the heck was all that maneuvering about back there?" I asked, trying to maintain a fairly steady voice. "Why didn't you set 'er down when we were over Low Lake? Why did you go back up in the fog?"

Magie grinned. "Well, see, it's an even ten seconds over the hump from Low to Bass Lake . . . I've shot hundreds of landings here with students. All I did was pull up the nose, count to ten, and drop 'er down. Bass Lake was right there."

"We darn near died of fright," I said. "Why land in Bass Lake instead of Low Lake, anyway?"

"Because," said Magie, "the trail out of Low Lake is a mile and a half, and it is only a half mile to walk out of Bass Lake. I saved us almost a mile of walking."

I glanced at Harry. He was wiping sweat off his face and shaking his head in disbelief. I doubt if any of us would have minded the extra walk.

The Very Important Person

He was a young man who had enjoyed some business success. He had traveled widely and was known to have spent a considerable amount of time in the outdoors, especially on the canoe trails of North America. However, he had never paddled the waters of the Quetico-Superior canoe country, a challenge that drew him to Ely, Minnesota.

Certainly, that afternoon when he first came into the newspaper office and introduced himself, he appeared genial and steady-eyed and offered a firm handshake. His wife, though very quiet, was pleasant. Both appeared fit from many miles on the canoe trails, and when he suggested a week-long canoe trip with Lil and me the following spring, it seemed like an opportunity for an enjoyable experience. A phone call to a magazine editor placed the trip in the realm of a story possibility that might have considerable readership value. During the winter an exchange of letters confirmed our plans. We looked forward to the trip with anticipation.

So on a warm, sunshine-washed June morning, we assembled our canoes, equipment, and food at Scott's Marina at Crane Lake.

A last check to make sure we had all of the necessary paperwork—camping permit, fishing licenses, and a map—and we were on our way.

In a sense, this was a celebration of sorts for Lil and me. We had not been on a canoe trip for well over a year while she was having surgery and extensive chemotherapy for a malignant ovarian cancer.

"Everything looks clear," said the Duluth oncologist after treatment and follow-up tests. "If you are planning to take that canoe trip, go right ahead. But don't overdo it."

"I don't know if I'm strong enough to paddle and portage at our old rate." Lil shook her head ruefully.

"Listen," I said. "If you can camp out and push the paddle even a little bit, we'll make it. Don't worry about portaging, I can handle the canoe and packsacks." After the fright with cancer, I was ready to accept any obligation just to get back on the canoe trails with my partner of more than four decades.

The trip was uneventful until we arrived at Curtain Falls, the frothy cascade thundering from Crooked Lake down to Iron Lake. Hours earlier, I had suggested we pause below the falls, unlimber our tackle, and pick up four fish for supper.

"You sure we can catch something here?" the V.I.P. asked.

"Never missed there yet," I said with complete confidence. In over thirty years of canoeing the border lakes, this was one spot where we never missed. But we did that day. We couldn't beg or buy a bite. The V.I.P. did not disguise his disgust, although his wife accepted our lack of luck with good humor.

At last we reeled up our lines and packed across the portage around Curtain Falls, coming out on Crooked Lake. A rumble of thunder behind us signaled the approach of a distant storm.

"Far end of the bay ahead and to the left, about two miles, there's an excellent sand beach and an adequate area to pitch camp," I pointed out. "I think we can make it before the storm hits."

"Yeah?" The V.I.P. said, his voice tinged with doubt.

Forty minutes later, we hit the sand beach, pulled up the canoes, and unloaded our gear. That's when things really began to change. First, the V.I.P. plucked a book from his packsack and moved down the shore to a convenient log, where he seated himself and began to read. His wife set about putting up their tent and spread out the sleeping bags inside, while Lil and I worked as a team getting our tent up and the campsite tidied. The V.I.P.'s wife helped us gather rocks to build a fireplace and set the grate in place.

"What's for supper?" The V.I.P. glanced up from his reading.

"There's a trail behind us that goes to Little Roland Lake . . . great spot to get some nice bass," I suggested. "I think we can make it before the rain comes."

"Uh-huh." He went back to his reading.

Lil and I began assembling our fishing tackle, and the V.I.P.'s wife got theirs ready to go. "Is His Honor coming with us?" Lil whispered. I broached the question.

"Oh, well, why not?" He yawned, stretched, and put the book inside their tent. He and I each picked up a canoe, and he took the lead down the portage, the women packing the fishing tackle and paddles.

His Honor was walking about fifteen paces ahead when he suddenly stopped and set his canoe down. I came up behind and stopped. "What's wrong?"

"Low spot full of rainwater," he said, pointing at a flooded section of the portage. "Would you mind carrying both canoes across . . . I'm wearing my new running shoes, and you're wearing old boots. I can go around through the woods and pick up the canoe on the other side."

This was certainly a new experience, but curious to see what might come next, I shrugged and carried my canoe through the puddle, then came back and got his. Lil had caught up with me by then. "What the heck are you doing?" she hissed angrily.

173

"Taking his canoe through the puddle. He didn't want to get his new running shoes wet."

"Oh, for heaven's sake. I've never heard of anything like that!"

"Me, either, but it's no big deal." I picked up the V.I.P.'s canoe and carried it across the water hole.

When we got to Little Roland Lake and pushed off, I pointed out where a few bass were surfacing along shore. "Try over there," I suggested.

"Yeah?" His Nibs seemed doubtful.

Lil and I headed for a familiar reef and immediately hooked a brace of smallmouth with surface lures. There was a splash behind us, and here were the V.I.P. and his wife. "The fish are all over here," he said.

Lil and I paddled away, heading for the opposite shore. Giving the V.I.P. credit where due, he could cast with reasonable skill. He picked up one nice bass but then reeled up when a loud clap of thunder sounded closer. By then we had a fourth bass, enough for supper, so we headed back. Again, I carried both canoes across the mud puddle while His Honor went around. Lil was fit to be tied. "You cut that out!" she snarled. "You're not a servant for these people!"

"I just want to see how far he'll go. It'll make a heck of a story some day."

To be absolutely fair, it was only the V.I.P. who had such a lofty opinion of himself. His wife was pleasant, energetic, and cooperative. Other than the canoe, she did all of the portaging and half the camp chores.

Back at camp, His Honor immediately returned to his book until the fish were cooked and supper was ready. One thing he did not lack was an appetite, although he did suggest that supper could have been cooked a little more to his taste.

Just before dark the storm hit, shook the treetops, and hammered the tents with sheets of rain. Toward dawn, it slacked off, but the sky remained overcast. "I didn't know we were taking a trip with royalty," Lil commented softly as we began rolling up our tent.

"Don't worry about it," I said. "I need the two of them for some photos for the magazine article."

Lil shook her head. "He makes me want to throw up."

"Well, just hang on. We've got only a couple more days to the end of the trip."

Following the storm, the bay by the campsite was quiet, but waves were showing far out in the lake. "We've got to get going." I addressed His Honor where he was sitting, reading. "When it starts to clear off, the wind will be kicking up pretty heavy out there."

"It isn't windy now." He turned a page in the book.

"Suit yourself," I said, "but we are heading out. You can follow us."

"I don't have a map."

"You don't need one. Just follow the left-hand shore."

As Lil and I rounded the first point, we could feel the wind velocity starting to build off the stern. In fifteen minutes, the sky was clear except for puffy cumulus, and we surfed down the lake on a stout tailwind. Occasional big combers caught us from behind, and we began to ship water. "Better pull in behind the next point and dump 'er out," Lil suggested.

A few minutes later, we rounded a wave-washed reef, curved into a quiet bay. Glancing back, we saw the other canoe coming, but dangerously low in the water. Their craft was a fast model for paddling but had a narrow beam and limited center height. Both the V.I.P. and his wife were now paddling furiously in an apparent attempt to keep their craft afloat. As they cut into the lee of the reef, a big wave washed over the gunwales and the canoe swamped. Fortunately, the water was only chest deep, and they waded ashore, dragging their half-submerged craft.

His Lordship was in a rather profane dither at this point. He yelled obscenities at the wind, the lake, his wife, and the world in general, and he jerked soggy packsacks from the canoe and hurled them angrily up on the shore. His wife scrambled to open the packs and get their sleeping gear and extra clothing laid out in the sun to dry. With the canoe turned over to drain, he fumbled around until he found his slightly damp book, swore a little more, and headed for a grassy spot where he could lean back and read. "Call me for lunch," he ordered.

His wife shrugged, picked up her casting rod, and sent a lure sailing out into the waves beyond the reef . . . and promptly connected with a two-pound walleye.

"Oh, ho!" Lil laughed, grabbing her tackle. "Feast today!"

His Majesty gave us a sullen look and went back to his reading. We managed one more walleye and a fair-sized pike, the trio providing six nice fillets, which were soon sizzling in the pan. His Lordship, Lil noted, was ever punctual at mealtime, but managed to vanish when dish washing began. Eventually the wind slacked off somewhat and we proceeded up the lake, making camp and whipping up supper from some packets of freeze-dried noodles and beef. He didn't care much for this either, but he ate his share.

It was on the Basswood River portages that things really began coming to a head. I had all the photos necessary for the magazine article and didn't really care what happened to the Royal Pain, but he wasn't through yet. Without question, he and his wife were strong paddlers. They surged ahead on the open stretches and arrived at the portages minutes ahead of Lil and me, where he would sit and stare at us with contempt.

"For people who claim to have a lot of experience, you two don't seem to be able to move a canoe very well," he noted. I didn't bother to explain that Lil tired easily. Indeed, I didn't care to talk to him at all.

We came to the last rapids below Upper Basswood Falls and began carrying across, His Nibs taking his canoe and nothing else. I had our canoe and a backpack. Lil stopped to rest a minute before crossing with a pack and the fishing gear. The V.I.P.'s wife had carried most of their packs across and was about to make her second trip with a light load. "Lil looks really tired," she whispered to me.

"She's recovering from a cancer operation," I replied, softly. "She's taking her time, doing the best she can do."

Without a word, the V.I.P.'s wife added Lil's pack to her second load and headed across; I had two Duluth packs and Lil had the paddles and tackle. When His Honor saw his wife with one of our packs, he let go a fine assortment of profanity and gave her a shove backward.

Lil and I had loaded our craft and were perhaps fifteen feet off the portage when I heard the V.I.P.'s wife yell at her husband, "Quit being such a jerk!"

I glanced back in time to see the Royal Pain wallop his wife with a loaded pack, knocking her to her knees. She scrambled up, brandishing a canoe paddle, and with fire in her eyes screamed, "You're still a big jerk!"

My first thought was to go to her aid, but when I saw the V.I.P. backing away from her, I assumed she had the situation in hand.

"Let's get out of here!" Lil exclaimed, driving her paddle blade angrily into the river. We shot upstream at a steady clip, coming out at the last portage below Upper Basswood Falls. Lil and I had made our first hike over when they caught up with us. His Honor put down his canoe and didn't say a word, just stared at me with kind of a sardonic grin.

During the trip he had occasionally inspected the map that I kept in my jacket pocket, since he was in unfamiliar territory. He carefully noted the penciled-in itinerary that would take us across Basswood Lake to Wind Bay, our last overnight camp. The following morning we planned to carry across to Wind Lake, make the final portage to Moose Lake, and paddle the last mile to the Boy Scout Base, where we could pick up transportation to my home, just a few minutes away.

As I completed my second trip across the Upper Falls portage, His Royalty was already preparing to push off with his wife in their loaded canoe. "I hope you don't mind, but I took the map out of your jacket pocket," he said, holding it up and smiling. "You paddle so much slower . . . we'll go on ahead and pick out a campsite at Wind Bay." His wife glanced toward us, then back up the lake in embarrassment.

Lil started to say something, but I gave her a look and shook my head.

"Sure . . . go right ahead," I said evenly. "We just can't paddle that fast."

The V.I.P. and his wife immediately struck out at a fast clip. He glanced back just once, noting we were preparing to push off, then their canoe went around a rocky point out of sight.

"The nerve of that guy!" Lil grumbled. "He took that map right out of your jacket."

"Forget it," I said. "Let's get going."

"I feel sorry for his wife, but I hate to think of camping one more night with that bozo," she said.

"We're not."

"What do you mean?"

"Watch."

The sun was setting in the west, a great ball of orange fire just above the tops of the spruce and fir. Rather than heading southeasterly across the lake after the other canoe, I aimed our craft up a channel to the west. "Instead of going to Wind Bay, we'll head over to Pipestone Bay . . . he'll never know where we went. Instead of coming in at Moose Lake, we can land at Fall Lake tomorrow morning and use a phone at one of the resorts to call home."

"Won't he look back and see which way we are going?"

"If he looks back, he'll be looking right into the sun . . . he won't see a thing."

Lil paused and glanced back. "I could have killed you when he had you carry his canoe through that mud hole."

"They say what goes around comes around," I said.

"What do you mean?"

"I mean he can paddle as hard as he wants and pick out any campsite he wants on Wind Bay, but he forgot one thing."

"What's that?"

"We've got all the food in our canoe."

Lil never did stop giggling as we paddled unseen along the west shore and into Pipestone Bay, cruising along for about an hour until we spotted an excellent campsite on a slight bluff. We beached the canoe, pulled out the packs, kindled a fire, and prepared a nice, quiet supper just for two.

Luck on the Redgut

It was one of those bright, windswept, high-barometer summer days in the north country. The sky was cerulean blue, the water shading from cobalt to ultramarine with whitecaps curling in huge crests across the broad width of Rainy Lake. We had gotten an early start from Bill Fontana's dock at Fort Frances and were well down the lake before the biggest waves began to pile up. Clamped on the left side of our fifteen-foot Grumman canoe was a sidebracket gripped by a purring three-horse Evinrude outboard. We had a long way to go over big water to our destination at the head of Redgut Bay, some forty-five miles to the east and north, and we felt the motor was critical to get us out and back in the one-week time frame we had scheduled for the trip.

Anticipating wave-caused problems, we used plastic liners inside our Duluth packs to keep our sleeping bags and duffle dry. Three-inch poles laid on the canoe bottom kept the packsacks above the water slopping in over the gunwales. In addition, I had my camera and films sealed in a separate plastic bag tucked underneath the rear canoe seat. Early on, we had taken a few photos around Fort Frances, but as the wind picked up, the camera went back inside the plastic bag, and we concentrated on watching and riding the waves, which were quartering off the stern in bigger and bigger volume.

About noon we hit Bear Pass at the mouth of Redgut Bay and churned our way along the lee shore with little difficulty except at the wide stretches opposite Baseline Bay and Crow Rock Inlet. It was afternoon when we crossed Spawn Inlet and threaded our way through swift currents to the boulder garden dotting the stream at the foot of the falls coming down from Otukamamoan Lake. On a sparsely wooded, grassy flat we pulled ashore. Our first order of business was to unload our Duluth packs and roll out and erect the tent. Our sleeping bags and foam mats were, thankfully, dry in their plastic covers. With sleeping gear inside the tent, we unpacked the cook kit and sorted out food for supper. It was then that I picked up the camera bag to get a picture of the camp and made a horrifying discovery: The plastic bag had sprung a leak inside the canoe and the 35mm camera was awash in water. Four rolls of color film in individual foil pouches were intact, but the camera was ruined.

Since this was a working trip and the photos were a necessity for a forthcoming magazine article, we had no choice but to return to Fort Frances to purchase another camera, come back, and start over. By sunup the next day we were on our way, traveling light, with just the canoe, motor, paddles, outboard gas, life jackets, rain gear, flashlight, and a lunch. It was July and warm. Anticipating more heavy seas, we stowed our clothes in plastic bags and wore our swimming suits. A stiff wind had already come up, more southerly than the day before, and we were bucking headwinds as we angled through whitecaps down Spawn Bay toward the main part of Rainy Lake. In the distance, we noted the cluster of cabins at Bob Lessard's fishing resort and made out a half dozen people standing on the dock waving at us. We waved back and kept driving into the waves as the lake got rougher and rougher. Even if we swamped, we reasoned, all that could happen would be that we'd get wet. But what a glorious ride we had! Sometimes the bow rose almost three feet off a cresting wave before slamming down in the trough, creating a flurry of glistening foam. Great puffs of white cumulus raced overhead. Seagulls wheeled and dipped on translucent wings, shrieking their delight.

We crossed Swell Bay, which was working hard to live up to its name, and motored through Little Rocky Narrows and then across to the U.S. side, where we were partially in the lee, droning steadily past Dryweed Island, Red Sucker Island, the cabins at Ranier, and on into Fort Frances. We docked in town, had a sandwich, located a camera shop, cashed some travelers' checks, and purchased a 35mm replacement unit for the one that had gotten drowned. This time I made sure the plastic bag had no leaks, then sealed the camera inside, and we started back.

Once again, when we left the relatively quiet U.S. shore, heading toward Redgut Bay, we got into huge waves. To put the situation in perspective, on much of big Rainy Lake someone on the water cannot see from one shore to the other. The lake simply stretches to the horizon and vanishes against the sky. It was a lonesome place in a canoe, especially with huge waves breaking from behind, some coming over the stern and threatening to swamp our small craft. Several times we stopped behind sheltering islands, pulled the canoe ashore, turned it over, dumped the water out, then continued onward. By afternoon, the wind had begun to drop, but we noticed the sun was becoming obscured by wisps of dark clouds, and we detected the distant rumble of thunder in the west. With growing concern, we droned on up Redgut Bay, watching the clouds edging ever closer.

"Let's duck into Lessard's for a cold pop and see what that storm is going to do!" I yelled at Lil over the drone of the motor. She gave me a thumbs-up sign, and I aimed the canoe bow across Spawn Inlet toward the resort dock. As we beached our craft and headed for the screened porch of the lodge, a grinning, suntanned Bob Lessard came out on the steps. "Come on in," he invited. We nodded and went into the cool interior.

"Couple of Cokes," I said.

"Where are you camped?"

"Up by the falls."

Lessard glanced out the windows at the darkening sky, shook his head.

"Looks like a lot of wind in those clouds," I noted.

"Not as bad as this morning," Lessard said. "It was really hammering our dock . . . couldn't even get our fishing boats out. And right in the middle of all that, a canoe with two people came down the lake, bouncing like a cork on the whitecaps. Bunch of us were standing on the dock trying to wave them in off the lake, but those dummies waved and kept on going right into the gale." He glanced out the window again. "Can you believe anyone could be that loony?" I looked at Lil, and she winked. I couldn't tell Lessard that we were the loonies.

Lightning split the sky from ground to clouds. Thunder cracked closer, and the first fresh wind gusts shivered across the bay. "Looks like it's going to be tough to get back to camp," I said, hoping that perhaps Lessard would invite us to stay until the storm went past or perhaps spend the night. He didn't pick up on it at all.

"If you're going to make it," he warned, "you better get going."

No doubt he had a camp full of people and would have been hard put to squeeze in two more. Reluctantly, we finished our pop and headed for the canoe, donned our rain gear and life jackets, gassed up the outboard, and pushed off. By the time we got across the bay and into the river channel, rain was pelting down, darkness descending, and the wind was moaning through the spruce tops overhead. I told Lil to get the flashlight out of the pack, keep it under her rain jacket, and flash it occasionally on the nearest shore so I could navigate without ramming into any rock ledges.

In addition, every lightning flash gave me a momentary fix on the scene, then total darkness would envelop us. Lil periodically aimed the flashlight at the shore, its yellow beam streaked with driving rain. In the narrowing channel, we hit swifter currents, the movement of the water pulling the outboard shaft first right, then left. There was one spot where we had to drive through a narrows between two ledges, throttle wide open. A mistake here and we could easily swamp and go rolling back down the current. I deliberately shoved that thought out of my head and concentrated on the rain-washed darkness ahead. Suddenly, the flashlight beam bounced off a sheer rock wall, dead ahead, almost within arm's reach. Throttle wide open, I carved away from the ledge, felt the canoe climb over the crest of the current, and eased into quieter water above.

More lightning flashes revealed the boulder garden just below our campsite. Throttled down, I threaded the canoe through the obstacle course, banging off a couple of rocks, but thankfully not hitting the prop. Lil kept sweeping the light ahead, and in the driving downpour we finally spotted our tent. With a prayer of thanks, I cut the power and paddled the last few yards to the shore. We pulled up the canoe, grabbed our bags, and ran for shelter. Inside the dark tent, Lil fumbled a moment, then struck a match and lit a big plumber's candle. I zipped the tent shut, then checked the new camera in the plastic bag. It was dry. Hastily, by candlelight, we stripped off our rain gear, wet boots, and soggy clothing. Lil flipped me a dry towel. Giggling like school kids, we rubbed our bodies briskly while sitting cross-legged on our sleeping bags. Reasonably dry, and still laughing, Lil tossed her towel to a corner of the tent, blew out the candle, reached up in the pitch darkness, and pulled me to her.

Even now, years later, whenever there is a storm at night, I recall vividly that trip up Redgut Bay, the smell of fresh rain, and the sound of wind and water drumming relentlessly on the roof of our tent.

Going Home

It had snowed, thawed, and frozen again and the Ely streets were icy. Lil was downtown, shopping, looking in all the storefronts filled with colorful Christmas gifts. Some jewelry caught her eye, and she paused by a store window, then took a step backward, and her feet slipped on the ice. She went down in a heap on the sidewalk. For a moment she was stunned. Several passersby and a store clerk rushed to help her up, and she managed to walk the two blocks to the newspaper where I was working, came in, and slumped heavily in a chair. Her face was white, and not just from the cold.

"You're not feeling well," I noted.

"Fell on the ice." She ran a hand over her neck and across the back of her head. "Landed on my back . . . it was very embarrassing . . . knocked me out for a few seconds."

I pushed my chair back from the word processor. "Are you O.K.? Want to go up to the clinic and get checked?"

"No." She was firm. "I just want to sit here a minute . . . get my breath back. I'll be all right." She lit up a cigarette and settled back in the chair. Ever since her first bout with cancer five years earlier, I had urged her, without success, to give up the cigarettes. Out of consideration for me, she bought a smoke filter, which she kept alongside her chair at home. In the car, she would crank down the window on her side. Cigarettes were something I never really learned to live with.

Lil looked wan and hurt. I repeated the suggestion that we go to the clinic. She shook her head. I closed up work early, and we drove home. That evening she was sore and stiff. Although I rustled up some burgers for supper, she just wanted to stretch out on the bed with a cup of hot coffee. She took a couple of aspirin for the pain, but passed a restless night.

The next day she was still in considerable pain, and I insisted we go to the clinic. She adamantly refused. The following morning saw no improvement. After considerable pleading, she finally agreed to visit the clinic. I made an appointment, helped her get dressed, and we drove to town. X rays showed she had cracked a vertebra in her lower back. The doctor confided that she would be in considerable pain for awhile, that she needed a lot of rest, that she should not attempt to lift anything. He prescribed some medicine for the pain; we picked it up at the drug store and then headed home. For the next few weeks, Lil didn't do much. I handled house chores and cooked the meals. Eventually, her back began to show signs of improvement, especially as spring approached, ushering in the walleye fishing season.

Jim Brandenburg, the *National Geographic* wildlife photographer who lives on the next road east, paid a visit. Jim allowed that he was jinxed and had never caught a walleye, although he lived in Minnesota most of his life. Lil shook her head with disbelief and invited him to go with us on opening day in mid-May. "We never miss getting walleyes," Lil affirmed.

"After a statement like that, we probably won't get any," I admitted, ruefully.

On Newfound Lake, a few miles east of our home, where a small stream empties in from Splash Lake, there is a gravel-bottom pool that sometimes contains walleyes in the early spring. To reach it, we had to cross a part of Splash Lake and beach the canoe. Lil was in the bow, Jim in the center, and I on the stern seat. When we hit shore, Lil jumped out and grabbed the bow piece.

"Just hold the canoe steady, we'll climb out," I said.

Instead, she gave the bow a heave to put it up on firmer ground, let out a cry of pain, and reached for her back. I swore under my breath. I knew that this was one thing she could not do with a cracked vertebra. But she quickly recovered and refused to acknowledge any problem, insisting we go on fishing. We walked down a short trail to the pool.

And oh, but the walleyes were there. It was a day when Jim Brandenburg broke his jinx. For two hours we cast minnows into the current and let them drift down into the pool. Lil took the first two fish. Then Jim got a nice one. And another. But Lil had a real touch that day. We stopped when we had a dozen: Jim got three, I got three, and Lil got six. We split the catch evenly, with Jim taking six home. He had company coming in and wanted to put on a walleye fry. Lil and I expected some relatives from the Chicago area, and our six walleyes would make a nice entree.

As we were parting, Jim inquired, "How come Lil caught as many as you and I put together?"

"She always does that," I replied. "It is something you have to get used to if you take your wife along. For some unknown reason, the fates that control fishing see to it that women and little kids catch most of the fish."

That night, Lil had difficulty getting to sleep. She put the hot pad on her back and took some pain pills, but tossed and groaned most of the night. However, after a few days, her back appeared better. We went fishing several times, and then in late August, along with Buddy, we took a canoe trip into Quetico Park. She agreed to paddle sparingly and only when she felt like it and to leave all the portaging and camp chores to me. We had a great time, caught and ate a number of fish, and spent a week listening to loons, watching eagles, seagulls, and beavers, and handfeeding the Canada jays and red squirrels. However, I noticed she tired easily, and we kept our fishing ventures short, no more than an hour or two on the water at one time.

That autumn we went fishing a few more times, but it was increasingly difficult for her to get in and out of the canoe. She made another trip to the clinic, and it appeared the vertebra was slowly healing up. As the leaves began to turn and the first frosts lay in blue fingers on the woodshed roof, she showed little interest in the coming hunting season, preferring to sit on the front porch in the sun and read, Buddy at her feet. If the weather was chill, she stretched out on her favorite recliner chair indoors and devoured mystery books by the box full. To keep the supply coming, I hauled a load about once every two weeks to the mall in Virginia, where they had a paperback exchange for used books. Winter came and we managed a few days of shopping in town, then drove to Illinois to spend Christmas with my sister, brother-in-law, and my ninety-eight-year-old mother.

Lil enjoyed Christmas immensely, laughed and joked and played with her grandnieces and grandnephews. But the twelve-hundred-mile round trip ride from Ely down and back taxed her endurance. She had a hard time getting comfortable in the car even with plenty of pillows for padding. Winter dragged on, with snow and subzero temperatures. Then came the inevitably longer days of March, when the sun began to arc higher into the sky each day and patches of brown began to appear where snow melted off the south-facing slopes.

Still, her back pain was not letting up, and I kept insisting she go back for another checkup with the clinic. The doctors were puzzled because the vertebra seemed to be healing up, but the pain remained intense. They made more tests and then expanded their X rays. A sober-faced doctor told me straight out that he didn't like what they saw. It looked like a malignancy, and an appointment had been made at the Duluth Clinic, equipped with more advanced medical facilities.

Lil accepted this without comment, but a cold finger of fear poked deep into my stomach. Our appointment was with Dr. James Krook, the oncologist who had successfully treated Lil five years earlier for ovarian cancer. We drove to Duluth, picked up our daughter Barb, drove up the circular ramp outside the clinic, left the car, and went inside to the waiting room. Through the large front windows, we could watch whitecaps rolling in the sunlight on Lake Superior. The beauty of the huge lake was in sharp contrast to a waiting room full of clinic patients, from kids to senior citizens, all hoping for a cure for some illness or other.

A nurse came out: "Mrs. Cary?" Lil nodded. We got up and went down the hall to Dr. Krook's office. When Lil, Barb, and I were seated, Dr. Krook brought out the latest X rays. His usual jovial, optimistic demeanor was missing. His jaw was tight, his eyes thoughtful. He held up the X rays so we could all see them. Her spinal column appeared all right, but it was to a series of nearby black spots he focused attention. He wiped a hand across his forehead and went into an explanation, one he had no doubt been forced to give many times over a long medical career.

"Much of the pain Lil has been experiencing does not come from the vertebra," he explained softly. "It comes from these." He pointed to the black spots. "These are malignancies that have invaded the liver and the lungs."

We sat stunned. I glanced at Barb. Her face was pasty white. Lil stared at the X rays as though looking right through them. I pointed to another black spot at the top of the spine, at the base of the skull. "What's that?"

"It is also invading her brain," Dr. Krook said simply.

I took a deep breath. "What can be done?"

"We could use radiation there . . . and chemotherapy treatment on the lungs."

I recalled how frightfully sick Lil had been with chemotherapy five years earlier. "What are the chances?"

Dr. Krook looked at Barb and me, then at Lil. "Perhaps we might make some headway with the lungs, but there is no treatment at all for the liver."

He looked us over for a moment. "If this was a member of my family—and I have gone through something like this at one time—I would say that if there is something you would like to do as a family, now would be the time to do it."

We sat shocked for a moment. "How much time do we have?" Barb managed in a choked voice.

"Perhaps six weeks," Dr. Krook said.

Six weeks? Our family had been together for more than four decades. In six weeks we would no longer exist as a family? Lil gave a sigh, stood up, thanked the doctor, and began putting on her coat. As we filed silently out the door, Dr. Krook gripped my sleeve and held me back. I stopped and glanced at him. There were tears in his eyes as he looked at me. "We are going to lose our friend," he said simply.

I stared at him, seeing a flesh and blood man with some uncommon skills who hated to lose a battle. "I don't think I could handle your job even if I had the training," I said softly. "But I thank you for the last five years . . . five extra years we had Lil with us."

Dr. Krook shook his head and turned away.

We dropped Barb off at her house in Duluth, then drove home to Ely, mainly in silence. Buddy was at the front door, barking and jumping up to get petted. Lil hung up her coat, then went quietly into the living room to relax in her favorite chair. I tried to put together a supper, but neither of us could eat. Somewhere I found a tape of Julie Andrews in *The Sound of Music* and put it on the VCR. It was one of Lil's favorite musicals, and as the songs began to unfold, the terrible tension in the room seemed to lessen. Lil smiled and stroked Buddy's head. It was almost as though the day had not happened. But it had. We talked no more about it.

April brought longer, warmer days. The snow vanished except for a few pockets in the shadowy part of the deep forest. Ice went off the rivers and began to crumble on the lakes. Although sometimes in pain, Lil was more her old self, laughing and joking about how she caught twice as many walleyes as Jim Brandenburg and I, recalling incidents from our fall canoe trip. We took some short walks in the spring sunshine, noting deer and wolf tracks in the mud alongside the road, stopping to watch woodpeckers chipping on dead aspen trees and chattering squirrels bouncing up balsam saplings just ahead of Buddy. At night we watched more films and talked about some of the great trips we had taken with our kids, our friends, our relatives. And people began dropping in. Our daughter Marge flew up from Houston, Texas. My sister, brother-in-law, mother, and cousin Bill and his wife, Patti, drove up from Illinois. Neighbors and former employees from our canoe outfitting days came by. And while these visits were all lighthearted, we knew each visitor had come to say good-bye.

The last week of April, the temperature shot up into the seventies. Seeking something to do, I started up the gas-powered cultivator and began digging up the vegetable garden, although I didn't know if I would plant one. Newly emerged balsam fir tips matched the bright green of spring grass. Leaves on budding aspen and birch began to appear. Lil came out on the back porch and motioned to me. I shut off the cultivator.

"Nice warm day . . . how about taking a canoe ride?" she asked with a grin.

"You feel up to it?"

"Sure," she laughed. "Let's see what the world is doing along the lakeshore."

I flipped a canoe onto the rack strapped to the car roof and shoved two paddles and life jackets inside. Lil called Buddy and we drove out the Fernberg Road to the Lake One landing, parking in the shade of some tall white pines. I carried the canoe and life jackets to the beach. Lil followed with the paddles, and Buddy raced from us to the shore and back, barking with sheer enjoyment.

We loaded up with Lil in her old spot in the bow, Buddy at her feet, and me on the stern seat. For the first half hour, we cruised slowly along the shoreline, observing the wet emerald-and-gold strips of mosses and lichens gleaming in the sunlight, the gray patches of reindeer moss blanketing the ledges. Here and there, a few small clumps of grayish snow still appeared alongside weathered blowdowns. Over it all, tall, regal white and Norway pines stood motionless against a deep blue sky. In the low spots, jagged jack pines reached out over last fall's brown cattails. All of this was reflected perfectly, upside down in the slick water, marred only when the bow of our canoe riffled through the mirrored scene.

At the west end of Lake One, I beached the canoe and stepped ashore on some huge, flat pieces of granite. "Want to walk over and look at the rapids on the other side?" I asked.

"No." Lil had her paddle resting on her lap. "I just want to sit here. You take Buddy across, come back, and tell me about it."

"I don't think Buddy will go with me." I walked a short distance up the trail and whistled. He stayed put in the bow, leaning against Lil's knees. So I walked across alone to the other side of the portage. There was a hot lump in my throat, and my eyes burned. Lil and I both knew this was our last canoe ride. We had paddled together in rain, wind, snow, and sleet, in sunshine and by moonlight. We had raised two daughters we were proud of, who had traveled many of the canoe trails with us. We had fished, hunted, and camped in some of the most beautiful scenery of North America.

Now it was coming to a close, and there wasn't one thing I could do about it. Slowly I returned to the canoe.

Lil grinned. "How do the rapids look?"

"Just like rapids," I said, trying to laugh.

We paddled back to the landing, loaded the canoe on the car, and headed home. Two weeks later, Lil died at sunset in her recliner chair. As was her wish, there was no funeral, no ceremony. A few days later, Barb, my cousin Bill, and I buried Lil's ashes at the base of a young Norway pine in the yard. We placed a new pair of moccasins with the ashes, an Ojibwa tradition to make the trip to Spirit Land easier, and said an Ojibwa prayer. In my will, I wrote that my ashes are to go alongside her under that same tree so, in some sense, we will both be nourishing something living.

When everyone had finally gone, Buddy and I went into the house. The emptiness was painful. Buddy curled up at the foot of Lil's chair as he had done for years, waiting for Lil to come home. But then, in a real sense, she is home.

As many old couples do, we had discussed this very situation a number of times. Lil pointed out that we come into this world with no written warranty as to how long we will be around and no appointed time to leave. We discussed the beliefs of her American Indian ancestors in an afterlife, a Spirit Land, a land of plenty, of warm sunshine somewhere toward the west.

"Whoever goes first," Lil insisted, "should put up the camp, build a fire, and put the coffee pot on."

Somehow I know the camp is already up, the fire is burning, and the coffee pot is on. Waiting. And I know that when I get there, it will be the best cup of coffee I ever had.